Our world fe᠎᠎᠎s.
We need simp᠎᠎
of our era. Linda Dillow offers bedrock truths fashioned in the crucible of deep suffering that brilliantly illuminate the path to maturity when our struggles feel overwhelming. Her gift for us is immense. She has not merely written a fabulous book; she has lived it and found the author of life true to His Word. So will you.

DAN B. ALLENDER, PhD, professor of counseling psychology and founding president of the Seattle School of Theology and Psychology

Linda's messages and life have mentored me for a very long time. She continues to do so in this new, wonderful book. The integrity and deep faith of her life shine through each page. She identifies the pain and struggles we all feel, yet she lifts us up to find a place of hope and peace in the presence of our Savior. You will cherish this book and read it over and over. Thank you, Linda, for this treasure of a book.

SALLY CLARKSON, bestselling author

Hope for My Hurting Heart is a treasure and a veritable spiritual feast! If you read one devotional book this year, make it this one. If you lead one book study with a small group, choose to go through this one. Even the heartbreaking stories of faith inspire, challenge, convict, and bless. Linda's seasoned faith invites us into a deeper intimacy with God and a trust in him that will stand the trials of life. This is Linda's magnum opus after a lifetime of writing substantive, enlightening books.

GARY THOMAS, author of *Sacred Marriage* and *Sacred Pathways* and teaching pastor at Cherry Hills Community Church

Where there are unspeakable pain, inconsolable grief, and unanswerable questions, there is a God who becomes our hope. Linda has been writing this message for decades. She has lived it and breathes it. I have "caught" this hope and love for the Lord through knowing Linda, and I pray that through the pages of this book you catch it too. He is the greatest of all hope!

>JULI SLATTERY, president and cofounder of Authentic Intimacy

Comforting and encouraging, this book is for every person who is suffering and needing hope. Linda writes with extraordinary compassion, authenticity, and humility. When your heart is hurting, let Linda lead you to hope. You will feel as though you have a treasured friend in your sorrow. There is no one I'd rather learn about hope from than Linda Dillow.

>BECKY HARLING, international conference speaker, leadership coach, podcast host, and author of *Cultivating Deeper Connections in a Lonely World*

Divine hope and practical help permeate the pages of this one-of-a-kind book written by this one-of-a-kind person, Linda Dillow. For decades, laughter filled the halls of her home as daughters Joy and Robin bounced in and out of its doors. (I know; I was there. Her family loved us well as we found respite under their roof during our sojourn of ministry living behind the Iron Curtain.) But now the halls of her broken heart echo pain in the face of unspeakable sorrow and suffering—both her daughters' and her own. Thank you, Linda, for articulating these eight Heart Skills learned in your fire of affliction and for paving the way for countless others to discover supernatural joy and lasting healing.

>DEBBY THOMPSON, author of *Pulling Back the Iron Curtain*, missionary with Cru Church Movements, and ambassador to women

In this book Linda Dillow—with the help and encouragement of Lorraine Pintus—openly, honestly, and vulnerably shares from real-life experiences in her personal life as well as what she has witnessed in the lives of others. Linda's solutions are never simplistic but realistic, practical, and always biblical. Her subtitle captures the essence of this book: eight Heart Skills to help you cling to God and never give up.

On a personal note, I've watched Linda walk through some of her most painful experiences with faith, hope, and love. Thank you, Linda, for practicing what you preach!

DR. GENE GETZ, professor, pastor, and author

NavPress

Published in alliance with Tyndale House Publishers

HOPE
— *for my* —
HURTING
HEART

*8 Heart Skills to help you
cling to God and not give up*

BESTSELLING AUTHOR OF *CALM MY ANXIOUS HEART*

LINDA DILLOW

with LORRAINE PINTUS

NavPress
Bold. Loving. Sensible.
NavPress.com

Hope for My Hurting Heart: Eight Heart Skills to Help You Cling to God and Not Give Up

Copyright © 2025 by Linda Dillow. All rights reserved.

A NavPress resource published in alliance with Tyndale House Publishers

NavPress is a registered trademark of NavPress, The Navigators, Colorado Springs, CO. The NavPress logo is a trademark of NavPress, The Navigators, Colorado Springs, CO. *Tyndale* is a registered trademark of Tyndale House Ministries. Absence of ® in connection with marks of NavPress or other parties does not indicate an absence of registration of those marks.

The Team:
David Zimmerman, Publisher; Caitlyn Carlson, Senior Editor; Danielle DuRant, Copyeditor; Lacie Phillips, Production Assistant; Julie Chen, Cover Designer; Cathy Miller, Interior Designer; Sarah Ocenasek, Proofreading Coordinator

Cover photograph of abstract painting copyright © by Djero Adlibeshe/Adobe Stock. All rights reserved. Cover photograph of gold texture copyright © by Studio Denmark/Creative Market. All rights reserved.

All Scripture quotations, unless otherwise indicated, are taken from the Holy Bible, *New International Version*,® *NIV*.® Copyright © 1973, 1978, 1984, 2011 by Biblica, Inc.® Used by permission. All rights reserved worldwide. Scripture quotations marked AMP are taken from the Amplified® Bible (AMP), copyright © 2015 by The Lockman Foundation. Used by permission. www.lockman.org. Scripture quotations marked AMPC are taken from the Amplified® Bible (AMPC), copyright © 1954, 1958, 1962, 1964, 1965, 1987 by The Lockman Foundation. Used by permission. www.lockman.org. Scripture quotations marked ESV are from The ESV® Bible (The Holy Bible, English Standard Version®), copyright © 2001 by Crossway, a publishing ministry of Good News Publishers. Used by permission. All rights reserved. Scripture quotations marked KJV are taken from the *Holy Bible*, King James Version. Scripture quotations marked MSG are taken from *The Message*, copyright © 1993, 2002, 2018 by Eugene H. Peterson. Used by permission of NavPress. All rights reserved. Represented by Tyndale House Publishers. Scripture quotations marked NASB are taken from the (NASB®) New American Standard Bible,® copyright © 1960, 1971, 1977, 1995 by The Lockman Foundation. Used by permission. All rights reserved. www.lockman.org. Scripture quotations marked NLT are taken from the *Holy Bible*, New Living Translation, copyright © 1996, 2004, 2015 by Tyndale House Foundation. Used by permission of Tyndale House Publishers, Carol Stream, Illinois 60188. All rights reserved. Scripture verses marked *Phillips* are taken from *The New Testament in Modern English* by J. B. Phillips, copyright © J. B. Phillips, 1958, 1959, 1960, 1972. All rights reserved.

Some of the anecdotal illustrations in this book are true to life and are included with the permission of the persons involved. All other illustrations are composites of real situations, and any resemblance to people living or dead is purely coincidental.

For information about special discounts for bulk purchases, please contact Tyndale House Publishers at csresponse@tyndale.com, or call 1-855-277-9400.

ISBN 978-1-64158-929-1

Printed in the United States of America

31	30	29	28	27	26	25
7	6	5	4	3	2	1

To my soul sister, Lorraine—who has prayed with me, pushed and encouraged me, and pulled this message of pain and broken dreams out of me. I love and appreciate you more than I can express. God thanks you, and His women thank you.

To my husband of over sixty years, Jody. Thank you for being a lover of God's Word and passing your love to me. Thank you for having two thousand books and commentaries and letting me mark them up—you know I treasure "real" books more than the internet.

CONTENTS

Does Your Life Hurt? *1*

CHAPTER 1 Hope *5*
CHAPTER 2 Love *23*
CHAPTER 3 Loss *43*
CHAPTER 4 Lament *61*
CHAPTER 5 Trust *81*
CHAPTER 6 Forgiveness *99*
CHAPTER 7 Encouragement *119*
CHAPTER 8 Praise *139*
Your Eight Heart Skills *157*

EIGHT-WEEK BIBLE STUDY *159*

Acknowledgments *235*
Notes *237*

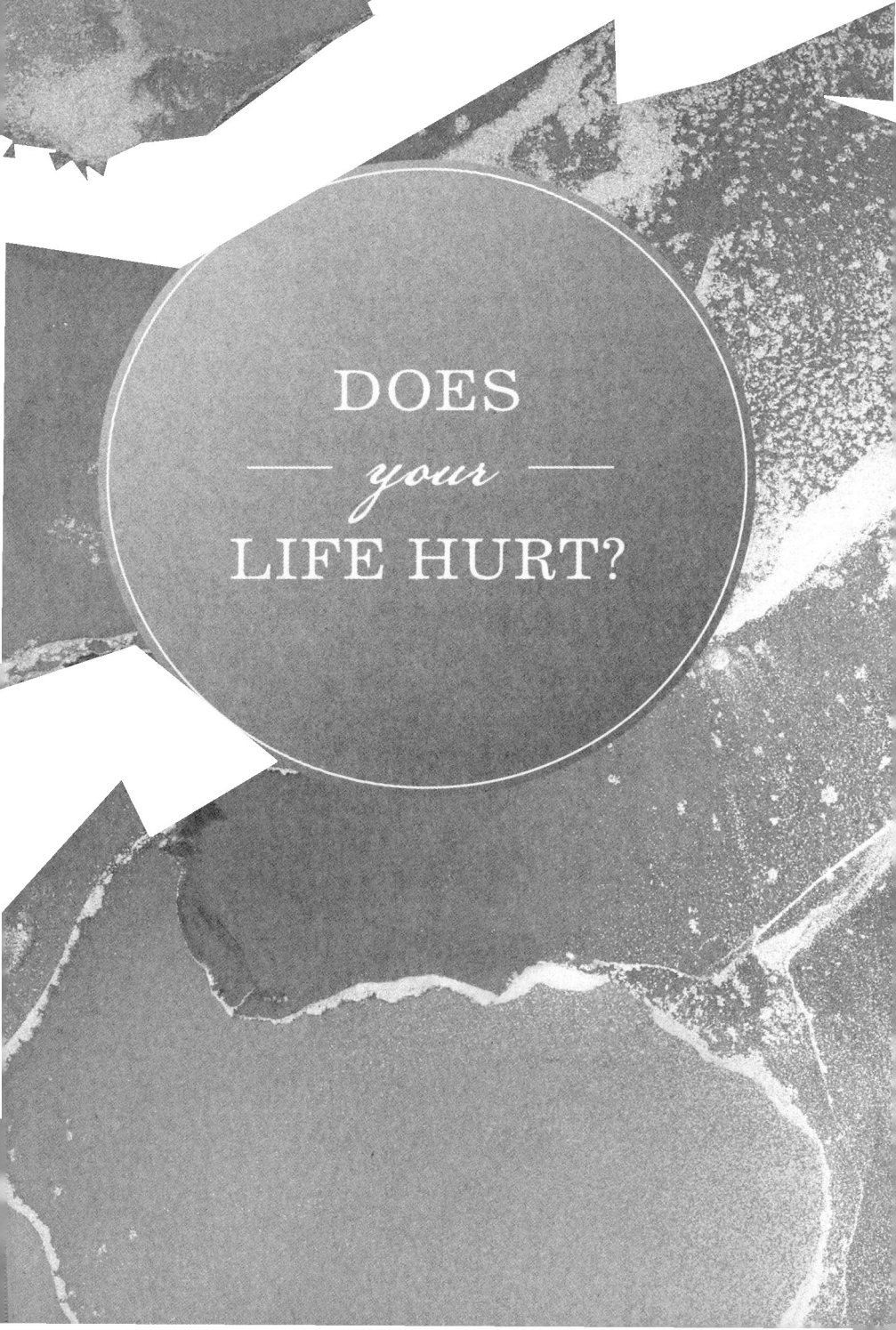

DOES *your* LIFE HURT?

*P*AIN.

My head hurts.

My heart hurts.

My dreams are shattered.

I have no words. The loss I feel is more than I can bear.

Does anyone know the way . . . to hope?

I wish God promised us a pain-free life. (One of my first questions for Him in heaven will be "Why, why, why didn't You make life pain free?") But Jesus said that in this life we will have pain, heartbreak, and trials.

So how do we deal with our pain? And, maybe more importantly, how do we walk with God in our pain? I believe that no loss I experience is beyond His understanding and that every heartbreak I face also breaks His heart. And I believe that, no matter how great my pain, He is the only one who can carry me through it.

When I was an eighteen-year-old college student, two pain-filled situations were ripping me apart inside. I didn't know where to turn. I had no strategies, no framework, no perspective to help me deal with the harsh realities of life.

Now I'm over eighty years old, and life's pain remains. In fact, the last few years have been the most painful of my life. But I have changed. After six decades of walking with Jesus, I have tools to deal with my pain, loss, and broken dreams.

When I was a young mom of three little ones, I learned about the Hebrew word *hokmah*, which is often translated "wisdom."[1] But it can also convey "skill."[2] I became captivated by that word. This kind of skill is infused with the wisdom inspired by God. *Hokmah*, which is used about three hundred times in the Old Testament, expresses a person's approach to life. It has been my goal throughout my life to intentionally live with *hokmah*, and in my thirties, I wrote this definition of who I wanted to become as a wife, mom, nana, missionary, mentor, writer, and speaker:

> Wisdom is taking the knowledge one has about God and applying it in a skillful way, that life might be lived as a thing of beauty.

Maybe you're thinking, *That sounds great, Linda, but how can I do this when life is falling apart and I can hardly put one foot in front of the other?* Oh, I understand! In these last years, I've lived a falling-apart life. But to my surprise, I found that even in great grief and pain, life can still be lived as a thing of beauty.

I wrote this book to share some of the *hokmah* God has taught me about walking through loss and pain. I call the tools I've found Heart Skills. Each chapter will teach you one Heart Skill, but you will get the most out of the Heart Skill if you apply it by doing the Bible study in the back of the book.

Let me ask you some questions:

~ *Are you so angry with God that you want to scream at Him?* There's a Heart Skill for that.
~ *Has someone done something so evil to you that you could never forgive that person?* There's a Heart Skill for that.
~ *Have you done something so terrible that you feel no one can love you, especially God?* There's a Heart Skill for that.
~ *Do you feel that the situation you currently face is hopeless?* There's a Heart Skill for that, too.

Each of the eight chapters holds hands with the one that follows to encircle you and fill you with the wisdom you need during hard times. I pray that as we journey together God will breathe hope into you.

Hope is where we begin because it's what we have lost and want to recover.
    Love is what we receive from God so we can walk through pain and loss.
        Loss is what we must face and acknowledge.
Lament is how we give voice to our pain before God.
    Trust is what develops as we cry out to God.
        Forgiveness is what trust equips us for.
            Encouragement is what we receive when we find our hiding place in God.
                Praise emerges because we see what God has done through this journey of loss and pain.

So turn the page, and let's begin with hope. After all, when your dreams are shattered and you are in deep pain, isn't God's hope what you need most?

CHAPTER 1

HOPE

[She] that lives in hope dances without music.
GEORGE HERBERT

Hope

Hope. Where are you? Are you hiding? I asked some women, "Do you feel hopeful?" They felt hope was hiding too.

> Hope? Mine flew out the window last week when my seventeen-year-old son said, "Just want you and Dad to know I don't believe all that Jesus stuff you do." Then I found porn on my fifteen-year-old son's phone.
>
> *Angela*

> I don't know if I'll ever find hope again. After twenty-three years of marriage, my Christian husband walked out the door. In one week, I lost my marriage, my home, and my dog.
>
> *Sarah*

> Before COVID I loved my job. Now I'm working from home, not loving my job, and struggling with the pain of a daughter who now wants to be a son. Hope is an illusion.
>
> *Kim*

Where do you go to find hope? The world around us promises hope in all sorts of places. I got a coupon for a moisturizer cream called "Hope in a Jar" that promised revival to my face. The ad copy even claimed that if I used the cream daily, I could live with optimism and be renewed with hope. Whoopee! I used my coupon, bought the cream, and—guess what? It didn't give me hope. It didn't even do anything for my wrinkles.

I'm wondering where you are today: hope-filled or hope-less? I find that many of us feel ourselves slipping down a "hope slide." The slide goes something like this:

Doubt (*Why would God let this happen?*)
    Discouragement (*How long will this pain go on?*)
        Despair (*I feel like giving up.*)
            Depression (*Maybe I will give up.*)

The bottom of that slide is such a horrible, gut-wrenching, heartbreaking place to be. A place where dreams and hopes are smashed. I know this firsthand.

My hope slide went like this:

~ *Christmas 2019:* Our daughter Robin called from New Jersey to tell us she had triple-negative breast cancer. Doubt set in: *How can this be, God? No one in our family has breast cancer. Robin is so healthy! She eats only organic food!*

~ *Christmas 2020:* Our oldest daughter, Joy—our super health-conscious girl, who made her own almond milk every night—called from California. "Mom, Dad, I have some hard news. The doctor thinks I might have liver cancer." Shortly thereafter, Joy was diagnosed with liver and pancreatic cancers. *Oh God, please no,* I cried out. *Two daughters with life-threatening cancer?*

One daughter had cancer on the East Coast, another had cancer on the West Coast. I was in Colorado, and I had to figure out some way to get to them. But the pandemic had shut down schools, churches, and businesses. Everyone wore masks. Schools were closed. Churches were closed. The government discouraged flying. For three days, I walked around my house praying and weeping. I praised God for who He is, but I could hear despair and depression call to me from the bottom of the slide. I fought against their pull. I had known hope in hard times before. I couldn't give up. I wouldn't give up. God had taught me in a crisis long ago as a new Christian that hope was something I had to grab hold of and hang on to with all my might.

My First Lesson in Hope

The year was 1964. I was a soon-to-be bride spending my summer away from Jody, my almost husband. He was working in a lumber mill in Oregon, and I was the director of a girl's camp in the mountains of Southern California. It was a different world then: no computers or cell phones. Can you imagine a life with no text messaging, FaceTime chatting, or even email? Because the camp didn't have a phone I could use, Jody and I communicated by old-fashioned snail mail, complete with a three-cent stamp. If we talked, I walked a mile down the mountain road from camp to a pay phone.

Jody and I both became Christians during our second year at university, and now we were to be married as our senior year began. The wedding invitations had gone out, and I was ecstatic to spend my life with this man I loved.

Then the letter arrived.

I read it once in shock and disbelief. Then read it again through tears. No! It couldn't be true! Jody had written that he doubted God and wasn't sure he really believed in Jesus. I'd fallen in love with Jody because of his passion for Jesus. Both of us had been revolutionarily changed by the love of Jesus. Now he was saying it was all a lie.

Talk about having your hopes and dreams smashed by one letter.

I put someone in charge of the camp, took my Bible, and climbed a mountain. As I walked, I screamed, "Help, God. Help!" Sitting on a rock, I begged, *God, speak to me. I feel so broken. How can I marry someone who denies You?* I opened my Bible to the book of Romans and began reading page after page, seeking wisdom from God.

When I reached chapter 8, these words jumped off the page:

> Hope that is seen is no hope at all. Who hopes for what they already have? But if we hope for what we do not yet have, we wait for it patiently.
> ROMANS 8:24-25

God's message to me from Romans 8 was this: *Linda, hope for what you can't see. Trust Me. I want to use you in Jody's life to help mold him and make him into that man of God you desire. Marry him, and serve Me together.*

While I didn't hear this message audibly from God, I felt it as a strong knowing deep in my spirit. God's instruction to me filled me with hope.

This kind of hope was new for me.

I grew up in a home with an abusive, alcoholic father who took his anger out on me. I knew little of God. For most of my life, my hope had consisted of wishful thinking.

Wishful-thinking hope boils down to "I hope for this because it will make me happy." Biblical hope is something completely different.

I love that the Greek word for "hope" in the New Testament, *elpis*, means "to have a joyful and confident expectation of good."[1] Biblical hope means we can anticipate good because that confidence is based on the nature and character of a good God, not on circumstances.

And so, at twenty-one, I learned my first lesson about biblical hope.

The next day when I walked to the pay phone and called Jody, the first words out of his mouth were "I sent a stupid letter. I don't mean a word of it. I don't know why I wrote it or sent it. Please don't read it!" I told him I'd already read it but it was all right.

I trusted God, and in that trusting, hope began to rise in me.

Biblical hope is one of the most powerful skills available to you to get you through life, and especially the hard times of life. But how do we form this kind of hope? I've learned that turning to the Word of God and listening to the Spirit of God create a sustaining hope in me no matter the circumstance.

The Word of God Gives Me Hope

Many years ago, my friend Dar gave me a Bible that was arranged so that it could be read in one year—a passage from the Old Testament, one from the New Testament, a psalm, and a proverb every day. This year, I'm reading through it for the twenty-fifth time. Again and again, Dar's thoughtful gift has breathed hope into my soul.

I love God's Word, all of it. But if I'm honest, every year my heart would sag when I came to Lamentations. Frankly, the book is depressing. Most years I read through it half asleep, skimming quickly over Jeremiah's endless laments. But I later discovered that in my skimming, I was missing a lot: the pain of this dear prophet, his literary excellence—and even the hope that shouts out loud in Lamentations 3.

When you read the first part of this passage, it's hard to miss Jeremiah's deep sorrow. You may wonder why you should read something that seems so depressing.

> He [God] has filled me with bitterness
>   and given me a bitter cup of sorrow to drink.
> He has made me chew on gravel. . . .
> Peace has been stripped away. . . .
> I cry out . . .
>   "Everything I had hoped for from the LORD is lost!"
>
> The thought of my suffering . . .
>   is bitter beyond words.
> I will never forget this awful time,
>   as I grieve over my loss.
> LAMENTATIONS 3:15-20, NLT

These are some of the most hopeless words in Scripture. I had to read "He has made me chew on gravel" several times. It's as if Jeremiah is stuck in a gravel pit and is so despondent that he picks up little rocks and gnaws on them for comfort. Jeremiah continually thinks of his misery, choosing to dwell on these painful thoughts.

But the change from verse 20 to verse 21 is like night and day. Suddenly, a switch is flipped in his mind with one word: *but*. And before our eyes, Jeremiah moves from sorrow to hope:

> *But* this I call to mind,
>   and therefore I have hope.
> LAMENTATIONS 3:21, ESV (EMPHASIS ADDED)

Are you leaning forward in your seat? Are you curious what this gravel-chewing man recalls that gives him hope?

Yet I still dare to hope
 when I remember this:

The faithful love of the LORD never ends!
 His mercies never cease.
Great is his faithfulness;
 his mercies begin afresh each morning.
I say to myself, "The LORD is my inheritance;
 therefore, I will hope in him!"

LAMENTATIONS 3:21-24, NLT (EMPHASIS ADDED)

Did you see what Jeremiah did? When he says, "I still dare to hope," he is arguing with his heart, turning himself away from the pit, and calling to mind wonderful, beautiful things of God.

Do you ever argue with your heart? Timothy Keller says, "We may hear our heart say, 'It's hopeless!' but we should argue back. We should say, 'Well, that depends on what you were hoping *in*. Was that the right thing to put so much hope in?'"[2]

Here is how Lamentations 3 has poured hope into me:

~ Hope does not come from a change in my circumstances; it comes from a change in my thinking.
~ My thinking changes when I say *but* or *yet* and call to mind who God is. My thinking changes when I dare to hope in Him today in the midst of my hard and painful heart hurt.

~ I paraphrase Lamentations 3:22-24 in a prayer something like this:

My God, I know You are full of loving-kindness, mercy, and faithfulness. So I say, "You are my portion; therefore, I dare to hope in You."

As you walk through dark days in your life, I hope you'll have the courage to say, *I call to mind, I remember, I dare to hope* what God's Word tells us is true about God. Like Jeremiah, I'm determined to rehearse what I know to be true. I'm going to recite what I know I believe. I'm going to dare to hope.

If you are like me, sometimes you just have to boldly preach to your heart! I rebuke myself and say, *Okay, Linda, enough now! No more of this dreary thinking. Lift up! Don't give in to your negative feelings. Fight against them! Don't wallow around in the dumps!* Then, after telling myself what not to do, I tell myself what to do: *Linda, put your hope in God! Remember all He has done for you in the past, how He has protected you and provided for you. You have hoped in Him in the past, and you can hope now!*

Hope makes my heart feel better. I had to preach to myself often in the last few years when the onslaught of hard situations kept tugging my heart down the hill toward hopelessness. But I knew God's Word, and His Word says I can fight. So I kept recalling the promises of God to find hope again.

My friend, rehearse the truth of Scripture to yourself. God's Word is filled with hope—there are over 7,700 promises in Scripture![3] Interpret pain through the lens of God's character, through the reality of His ultimate mercy.[4] As you do, God's hope will stir in you.

The Spirit of God Gives Me Hope

As a college student and new Christian, I was taught to be filled with the Holy Spirit. I believed God's Spirit worked in me, but my personal relationship was with Jesus, my Savior, and God, my Father, not really with the Holy Spirit. I've now come to know the Holy Spirit as an intimate friend, and I'm so grateful for His counsel and comfort in my life.

Many people are hesitant to connect personally with the Holy Spirit because He is mysterious—He seems less knowable than Jesus, my Savior, or God, my Father. My friend Kate struggled with this. When I asked her if she talked to the Holy Spirit, Kate said, "I couldn't. *Holy Spirit* sounds like a title, not a name. It's not friendly."

"Oh, but you're missing such joy!" I told her. "Jesus sent the Spirit to live in you, to be your comfort, your hope!"

Kate's words sent me on a search because I know she is not alone in keeping the Spirit at arm's length. Here's what I found:

~ In the New Testament, "spirit" is the Greek word *pneuma*, which can also mean "wind" and "breath." The related verb form means "to breathe" or "to blow."[5] The Spirit is like the wind: invisible, immaterial, and powerful.

~ Jesus was sent to earth and given a body. Jesus sent the Holy Spirit to earth without a body—and my body, and your body, would be His body and home.

~ Almost every mention of the Spirit includes the word *holy*. The beautiful thing is that *holy* is more than a reference to the Spirit's deity; it's also a reference to the nature of His work. He is called holy because He was sent to reveal the Father and Son and do His holy work in us and through us.

This makes me want to fall to my knees in worship! Think with me, my friend, about this incredible truth: God sent His Spirit to live in you and to be with you as your personal comforter and hope. Are you as overwhelmed by this thought as I am?

When Jesus told His followers He was going to send the Holy Spirit to them, He called the Spirit the *paraclete*, or comforter (John 14:16). Jesus wanted to leave no doubt about the many-faceted roles the Holy Spirit plays: comforter, counselor, helper, teacher, encourager. Each of these names, ministries of the Spirit, is unique—and each is available to us as the blessed Holy Spirit dwells within us.

That is what Terry Wardle, a leader and teacher of others, discovered. Terry had lost hope, and he was contemplating the unthinkable—taking his own life. But this verse literally halted his plans:

> Now may the God of hope fill you with all joy and peace in believing, so that you will abound in hope by the power of the Holy Spirit.
> ROMANS 15:13, NASB

Terry was not the only one ministered to by Romans 15:13. He later shared this verse with John, a man who was also ready to take his life. John, too, turned from desperation and found hope. Terry says,

> Then we went to the Lord in prayer and asked Him to make these promises a deep inner conviction within John's spirit. . . . The Spirit instilled hope in John and strength to hold on.

Such hope is not the result of positive thinking. It comes as a transaction of the Holy Spirit in the life of the believer. It pushes back the clouds of gloom and pessimism, bringing the light of God's promised deliverance and restoration.[6]

Oh, the life-giving power of the Holy Spirit, who is our blessed hope giver! If you need hope today, simply say to your friend, comforter, helper, and counselor who lives within you, *I hurt so much. Will You please, Holy Spirit, pray for me?* (See Romans 8:26).

My Declaration of Hope

Early in 2020 after our daughter Robin's cancer diagnosis, we packed our bags to travel from our home in Colorado to her home in New Jersey to be with her during chemo treatments. But because of the worldwide pandemic, life was far from normal. The phone rang. Robin's husband, Miku, told us not to come: "Robin is in quarantine, and the doctor says no one is allowed in our house, not even you."

My heart fell. I couldn't go to be with my daughter who needed me? I did what any self-respecting mother would do: I sat by the suitcases and sobbed until there were no tears left. A few weeks later, our sweet Robin had a horrible reaction to her chemo. Her blood levels tanked, and she was taken by ambulance to Memorial Sloan Kettering Cancer Center in New York City. No visitors were allowed. I prayed and called out to God continually, but discouragement was tugging me down that wretched hope slide.

I forced myself to run to God's Word and to the Holy Spirit, where hope was available. I turned to 2 Corinthians, where the apostle Paul had given me hope and encouragement many times.

In this, his most personal book, Paul intimately shares about a supernatural encounter with God as well as about deep discouragements with people and circumstances. Paul was in a hard place, but his real, raw words lifted me to hope:

> We are afflicted in every way, but not crushed; perplexed, but not despairing; persecuted, but not forsaken; struck down, but not destroyed.
> 2 CORINTHIANS 4:8-9, NASB

Twice in chapter 4, Paul says strongly, *I never give up! I never give up!* As I read those words, I felt as if they were written just for me. So, by the power of the Holy Spirit, I joined the apostle and said out loud for God and anyone else to hear, "I never give up!"

One morning I was on my knees in my living room worshiping with my cancer surrender song, "New Wine" by Hillsong Worship. Through tears, I thanked God for plowing new ground in my life, for cutting my heart to pieces, even though I hated it. I asked Him to bring new wine out of this crushing winepress of pain, even though I'd never raised my hand and volunteered for it.

I thought again of Paul's encouragement that I should not look at the seen but at the unseen: "We live by believing and not by seeing" (2 Corinthians 5:7, NLT). This was the same message God had spoken to me almost six decades earlier when God had given me my first lesson in hope.

Encouraged, I prayed:

> *Abba, don't let my eyes stay on the circumstances. Help me. I'm so scared. I beg You for Robin's life. For Joy's life. Oh, my*

precious daughters. I love them so much. I ask You that they live, but I give them, my treasures, into Your loving hands. I want to live by believing and not by seeing.

My pain felt all-consuming, relentless, and so agonizing that I had no words for it. I knew I had to align myself with God, to let His perspective be my perspective. He promises hope in the darkest of circumstances.

I took God at His Word and took a stand for hope. I call it my Declaration of Hope.

Linda's DECLARATION OF HOPE

I got out a yellow legal pad and a pen and with tears wrote these words on the blank page:

- ~ *GOD, DON'T WASTE MY PAIN!!!* My Lord, my prayer is that You will be glorified through my pain.

- ~ *FATHER, USE THIS PAIN* to build perseverance, character, and hope in me. Use my pain to make me more like You (Romans 5:3-5).

- ~ *ABBA, COMFORT ME* so I can comfort others (2 Corinthians 1:3-4). Let me nestle down in Your soft comfort so completely that it will flow through me to others in pain.

As I walked through the three years of my personal pandemic, watching my two daughters struggle with life-threatening cancer, I shared my Declaration of Hope with many hurting women, including some precious women in war-torn Ukraine. How my heart bleeds for brave women like Olga, Oksana, and Lena, who suffer long, not knowing if husbands, sons, fathers, or friends will come home from the battlefield; who pray and weep; who always make room for five, ten, or any number of others around their table.

After I shared over Zoom about my hope slide and writing my Declaration of Hope, Lena wrote her own declaration. As you read her words, think of her in Ukraine, praying and weeping before God, sweeping and cooking for others.

Lena's DECLARATION OF HOPE

~ Lena wrote out Romans 12:11-13: "Never be lacking in zeal, but keep your spiritual fervor, serving the Lord. Be joyful in hope, patient in affliction, faithful in prayer. Share with the Lord's people who are in need. Practice hospitality." Then she prayed,

Oh, Lord, it is so hard to see so much suffering. Help me be comforted by hope in You, that I don't get weary in fervor when I'm so saddened seeing people's sufferings. Father, what do You want me to learn in this horrible tribulation? Help me be patient. Help me be constant in prayer for the country and people, to intercede for those perishing. Help me participate in the needs of Your saints so that the world will see love among Your children.

I also shared my Declaration of Hope with the women who were involved in a pilot Bible study to test the material in this book. One of those women, Kyra, created her own declaration.

Kyra's DECLARATION OF HOPE

~ I needed a Declaration of Hope because I learned of a family member's bad choices that even landed on the news. This situation won't go away anytime soon—the sorrow and sadness my mother and father are dealing with deeply grieves me. The second reason I need a Declaration of Hope is because I'm leading a women's mission team to Thailand for the first time—this is beyond me for sure! But with God's help . . . I will hope for another nation. Here is my Declaration of Hope:

Precious God/Holy Spirit,
Help me always remember that You are with me in any and
all tribulation.
Help me know I can smile at the unknown future because
You are good.
May I lift my eyes to You, morning by morning, day after day,
through noontime and to the setting sun.
You are forever present, Emmanuel.
Forever faithful, forever good.
No matter what storm may come, no need to anticipate with
fear—just hope!
My God is here, Holy Spirit, the comforter and counselor.
When fear gives in, when darkness roams, my God is here.
Emmanuel, God with us, living inside.
I choose to put my hope in You, faithful God. Holy Spirit,
who gives breath to my doubt and awakens me—come and
blow, come like the wind and show Your power and help me
in the hard, hopeless-to-man situations!

Lena's and Kyra's Declarations of Hope encourage me. It's been several years since I wrote my Declaration, but it continues to be a daily compass of encouragement to me. My other source of hope is to soak in God's love. When God's love fills my heart, anxious thoughts evaporate. I am at peace. Where would I be without the love of God?

Do you receive God's love for you in your heart? Oh, my friend, this is a special gift for you when you need hope. Turn the page, and learn how the love of God can fill you up so you can face whatever trial is before you.

Heart Skill
A DECLARATION

Ask God and the Holy Spirit to help you create your own Declaration of Hope. Your declaration can take any form — words based around a Scripture, a song, or a prayer. It can be related to a symbol or a picture you paint. Be creative! The point is to have something concrete that grounds you in God's hope that you can refer to again and again.

CHAPTER 2

LOVE

*God and love are synonymous.
Love is not an attribute of God,
it is God; whatever God is, love is.*
OSWALD CHAMBERS

Love

I AM CONVINCED THAT THE GREATEST WAY to pour hope into your hurting heart is to sink deep into the love of God and to know—really know—the height, width, and depth of God's tender love for you. When God's love fills and overwhelms you, you know you are not alone and that, by His power, you can face whatever is before you.

Let me ask you a question.

Does God loving you excite you? Does the thought of His love set your feet to dancing?

For many women, it doesn't. Why? Could it have something to do with the word *love*?

In our English language, we don't have words to differentiate between different kinds of love. We say, "I love my child." "I love my dog." "I looove how my dark sea salt caramel chocolate bites melt in my mouth." The word *love* has been watered down to the point that when I say "I love God" or "God loves me," we're not sure what that really means.

I love the Greek language in which the New Testament was written. This language has words to describe the exactness of God's love for you and me. The Greeks had some different words for love—*phileo* to describe friendship love and *eros* to describe sexual love, for example. But Christians needed a different word to describe the revolutionary, unconditional, sacrificial love that Jesus showed us as He expressed the very heartbeat of God. They employed the word *agapē*, which was seldom used in that day, and gave it new meaning.[1] This lay-down-your-life agapē love was equivalent to breaking the sound barrier. Because of Jesus' love for us, we can all soar into new dimensions of love.

Agapē love is action oriented. Agapē love pursues, protects, hopes, and perseveres. Jesus' agapē love reaches toward you with outstretched arms, but it is a love that respects your free will. Jesus waits until you give permission, until you agree to open your heart and receive what He has for you.

First Corinthians 13 is known as the Bible's love passage. It's often read at weddings—it was read when Jody and I were married over sixty years ago. One commentary says that 1 Corinthians 13 is really "a character sketch of the Lord Jesus."[2] When we substitute Jesus' name for the word *love* in verses 4 through 8 and identify to whom His agapē love is directed, we may find ourselves startled with a fresh perspective.

Jesus is patient with you. Jesus is kind to you.

Jesus does not keep a record of your wrongs.

Jesus always protects you, always believes in you, always hopes for you, always perseveres in His love for you.

Jesus never fails you!

God's Love? Experience It!

If you are in pain, you may feel numb or even dead inside. You can't feel the expansive agapē love in which Jesus longs to enfold you. But let me say this clearly: *You are not dead.* You are alive! I know, you hate pain. So do I. But perhaps your pain is creating an opportunity for God to show you something new about the way He loves you. As C. S. Lewis says, "God whispers to us in our pleasures, speaks in our conscience, but shouts in our pain: it is His megaphone to rouse a deaf world."[3]

Having two daughters in cancer-treatment programs at the same time made me numb. All I knew was that I needed to feel God's love. I ran to Him and cried, "My God, I must sense You wrapping Your love around me and holding me tight."

For months, I'd been quoting Psalm 63:8, "My soul clings

to you" (ESV). I'd been clinging to God, wrapping my arms around Him in a desperate attempt to soothe the ache in my soul. But when I first heard the song "Just Be Held" by Casting Crowns, I was undone. As I meditated on the words of the song, God showed me that I didn't need to cling to Him for dear life, as I had been doing. No. He wanted me to stop striving. To sigh, lean back, and be held by Him. For me, this was a deeper understanding of God's love.

Maybe you think, *That's fine for you, Linda. But God doesn't love me. If He really loved me, He never would have let this horrible thing happen.* Oh, friend, God does love you. His open arms wait for you just like they did for me. Listen to truth:

> I am convinced that neither death nor life, neither angels nor demons, neither the present nor the future, nor any powers, neither height nor depth, nor anything else in all creation, will be able to separate us from the love of God that is in Christ Jesus our Lord.
> ROMANS 8:38-39

Or I could paraphrase God's Word this way:

> No! Neither cancer nor dementia, neither job loss nor home loss, neither the death of a child nor betrayal by a loved one—no evil person, no hurricane, no wildfire can separate uniquely created you from the love of your Abba Father.

Can I encourage you to open your heart, let down your barriers, and experience His love? It's a love like no other, a love that comforts and heals, a love that is supernatural.

Oh, friend, I so want you to know firsthand the deep, deep love God has for you. But you can't know this love unless you open your wounded heart and receive it. Only receiving His love will heal your hurting heart. This is what the Adoration Gals learned.

It's Wednesday morning. Six women, each facing painful situations in her life, sit around a wooden table with open Bibles and notepads before them. They have come to seek God and to pour agapē love over one another.

I am a member of this group. We call ourselves the Adoration Gals.

Two women are therapists. One is a biblical counselor. Lorraine (my soul sister who is writing this book with me) and I are writers. And then there's wise Valerie, who will share her story in the last chapter of this book. We do not come to chitchat about the weather. We are God chasers who are determined to experience God's presence in our lives. Brother Lawrence showed us how to practice the presence of God in his book by that name, but he was a monk! We Adoration Gals want to know how to do this as busy, scattered women in the twenty-first century.

One woman has a beloved daughter with mental-health issues who threatens suicide weekly. Another woman just went through a painful divorce because her husband of four decades found someone else he liked better. Most of us have a life-threatening health issue or have a loved one who does. We range in age from forty-seven to eighty-two (I am the oldest).

As a group, how do we deal with our pain? We study God's Word. We pray, love, and encourage one another. We run to God. But we are not satisfied with merely knowing about God. We want to experience Him. To encounter Him. We believe in God's love, but we also want to receive His love.

We've read several books about receiving God's love because being filled first with His love is what enables us to go through hard times with grace and *hokmah* wisdom. We've learned that when we bring our pain before God and are honest with Him, we open ourselves up to receiving His love in a deeper way.

Valerie: Light

God often soaks me with love through light. He daily gets my attention as light appears in a thousand glorious forms. Sometimes it's the way the morning sunrise dances on a single blade of grass. Or a chorus of sunrays that crescendos through a grove of trees. In these moments, God whispers gently, *I know you are hurting, child. But I am here. I am the Light of the World. Take My hand, and follow Me.*

Dar: Meditation and the Word

I receive God's love each morning as I quiet my spirit, close my eyes and gaze upon the One who is love and sweetness itself. I hear Him say, *I love to be with you, My beloved!* My favorite book is *Trusting God: Even When Life Hurts* by Jerry Bridges. God has revealed His love through my pain.

Elena: Emotions

For years, I've deeply studied God's Word. I use my mind a lot, so I love it when I receive God's love through deep emotion. I take a walk, breathe in the fresh air, listen to worship music, talk to God, and then enjoy a really good cry. God loves me deeply in those moments.

Lorraine: **Solitude and Surrender**

I receive God's love in solitude. First, I create outer solitude by shutting my office door. The click of the latch is my signal to mentally detach from the outer world. Then I find inner solitude—I lay face down, spread eagle, on my furry, white rug and whisper, "Abba Father, I need You. Fill me with Your love. Cleanse my motives and direct my steps for this day."

Diane: **Worship**

I go to God like a little child, feeling a bit unworthy. As I listen to worship songs about His greatness and majesty, I refocus my scattered senses upon my Father. The music pulls me to a heavenly place. I'm fully there but also fully here. I'm learning to worship in my pain, and it is a beautiful thing. He loves me when I'm laughing or weeping.

Do I hear you saying "I want to join the Adoration Gals"? Yes, we are a special group who love God and each other. I love what Diane said about worshiping in pain. These special friends have upheld me in the midst of my pain and helped me keep my eyes on who God is. During my years of loss, time on my knees before my Abba became my place of refuge.

Where I could be quiet when my head, heart, and world were racing.

Where I could weep and my soul could be understood.

Where I could receive God's love but at the same time ask, *God, will I ever feel delight again?*

Being immersed in God's divine love transforms a person. It's not enough to just say we are Christians or that we believe in Jesus. Only the experience of God's love is transformational. Sadly, many have missed this. One of my favorite authors, A. W. Tozer, says that "most of us who call ourselves Christians" do so on the basis of belief rather than experience: "We have substituted theological ideas for an arresting encounter; we are full of religious notions, but our great weakness is that for our hearts there is no one there."[4]

I'm so glad someone is there. There is a God who longs to love us in our times of pain, who is as close as our next thought, and whom we can know intimately. This is what I long for for you during your time of loss or shattered dreams—for you to truly know His deep love for you.

Becoming a Lover of God: Let's Learn!

When we talk about love, we usually immediately think of loving God and loving others (the two greatest commandments in the Bible). That's because as Americans we are doers. We like doing. It makes us feel good. But God doesn't want us to start with doing. He wants us to start with receiving—receiving the love He eagerly longs to give: "First we were loved, now we love. He loved us first" (1 John 4:19, MSG).

So we begin by receiving from God. But are we to just keep His love inside us and selfishly hold on to it? Of course not. As God fills our hearts with His love, we are to reciprocate by pouring devotion and adoration back to the God who loves us. Mark 12:30 says, "Love the Lord your God with all your heart and with all your soul and with all your mind and with all your strength." Jesus tells us that this is the greatest commandment (Mark 12:31).

David

King David was called a man after God's own heart because he loved God and sought Him eagerly (see 1 Samuel 13:14). In Psalm 139, David writes a very personal love letter to God. How personal? In these twenty-four verses, David uses the first-person pronoun (*I*, *me*, or *my*) forty-eight times. He uses the second-person pronoun (*you* or *your*) thirty-four times. It's as if David is looking into the very depths of his own heart and disclosing it while also looking deeply into the heart of God.

Let me show you just a few verses:

> O LORD, you have searched me and known me!
> PSALM 139:1, ESV

Yada ("to know") is the Hebrew word often used for an extremely intimate knowing. What David describes is not a surface knowing but rather a deep seeing and exploring by God, and David's response is holy awe. David is saying, *God, you have seen inside my very soul.* Then David says this to God:

> You see me when I travel
>   and when I rest at home.
>   You know everything I do.
> You know what I am going to say
>   even before I say it, LORD.
> PSALM 139:3-4, NLT

The spawning of raw thought and emotion occurs before actual words form on lips. It's in this place, the prebirth of words, where God knows David.

You go before me and follow me.
You place your hand of blessing on my head.
PSALM 139:5, NLT

Charles Spurgeon beautifully expresses David's words this way: "Our heavenly Father has folded his arms around us, and caressed us with his hand."[5]

But did you know that this king and poet had a messy life? Perhaps you have problems with an adult child. David's son stalked him and tried to murder him. How painful is that? David committed adultery with Bathsheba and then murdered her husband. That's on my list of what I consider to be really bad sins. Fortunately, he didn't just sit in his sin; he wrote two beautiful psalms to God to express his deep repentance and sorrow over his actions (Psalms 51 and 32).

David's words give me hope that I can enter a deep intimacy of love with my God no matter the pain or messiness of my life! I have used David's words in Psalm 139 to write my own love letter to God, and it's been a blessing and encouragement to me.

Now I want to tell you about a modern-day seeker after God, my dear friend Juli.

Juli

Juli came to me and said, "Linda, I love God with all my soul and mind and strength, but I don't know how to love Him with all my heart. Will you teach me?"

I could hardly speak. Juli is a psychologist and a brilliant mind person, and she recognized that bringing her heart to God was more difficult. I envisioned God singing over Juli with delight and declaring, "Yes! This is the kind of passion that I desire in my daughters."

So Juli and I went to my favorite "alone with God" getaway,

Praise Mountain, a prayer and fasting hideaway in the cleft of a mountain pass about an hour's drive from my home. There, in a rustic cabin surrounded by towering pines, we talked and prayed for hours about what God was inviting Juli toward in pursuing heart-deep love for Him.

Juli had just completed the P90X workout program, a set of twelve high-intensity workouts for ninety days straight. The goal of the program is to totally reshape your body. (Considering that my main exercise program involved walking Cali, our golden retriever, for a mile every day, I was very impressed with Juli's discipline.)

"Linda," she said, "I got up at 4:30 a.m. for ninety days to spend ninety minutes buffing my body." (And her body was buffed!)

What she said next made me choke back tears. "I'm asking, what would happen if I did an intense spiritual workout with God? What if I commit to spend ninety minutes every day for ninety days with God so I could reshape my 'spiritual body'?"

How Abba Father loves a heart like Juli's!

Juli and I got on our knees and worshiped the God who reshapes us. I prayed over her and asked the Lord to paint a picture for her of what it looked like for her to love God with all her heart. I went to bed, but Juli stayed up all night, seeking her God.

During the wee hours of the morning, the Holy Spirit came and ignited in Juli a new, burning love for God that was so personal and intimate she could hardly speak of it. Today she doesn't only love God with her soul and mind—she is also a heart person who loves God passionately.

Juli's ninety-day spiritual reshaping plan inspired me to step up my own devotion to God. I asked God to show me what a plan might look like for me as a grieving woman. After all, this kind of spiritual and relational intentionality can feel exhausting when we are in pain. And yet I knew that loving God in my pain would reshape me, sustaining my heart and soul to love and be loved no matter the circumstance.

"GO TO THE NEXT LEVEL" SPIRITUAL PLAN
Linda, an empty nester in pain

1. Continue reading my *One Year Bible*. (This is a practice that provides stability in my life.)
2. Study the Psalms and ask God to help me learn to lament.
3. Read two books on lament: *A Sacred Sorrow* and *Dark Clouds, Deep Mercy*. Ask God to speak to me about how I can trust Him in this time of great pain.

I asked other women in different stages of life what a spiritual program would look like for them.

Alix, a mother with three young children

Between running my three kids around to school and sports and working full time, I don't have a lot of extra time to spend with the Lord. Also, as someone who loves to check off a to-do list, my plan can't just be an item on my to-do list. It needs to be an all-day exercise, including Jesus in every step of life. It's the whispers for patience and energy when I am up in the middle of the night with a child or when my kids are fighting in the back seat of the car on the way to school. It's also quick words of praise to God for the sunshine or when I get a rare quiet moment. Most importantly, it's learning to stop in the middle of the overwhelm and keeping my mind set on what's most important—God!

Kim and Tracy, worship walkers

Two close friends wanted to grow in deeper intimacy with God. Their program took the form of a one-hour walk together twice a week. Kim shares,

> We start our walk praising God. We go back and forth and thank Him for everything we can think of. The last part of the walk, we talk to God about whatever is on our hearts. We are very honest—and confidential—with one another. We pray for each other's problems and pain. After every walk, I feel closer to God and closer to my dear friend. And I'm pretty sure many world problems have been resolved as a result of our simple praises and prayers.

When we love God with our whole being, His love fills us up and naturally spills out. We are so filled to the brim that we can't help but spill over and love others.

Becoming a Lover of Others: Let's Learn!

Jesus said that the second greatest commandment is to "love your neighbor as yourself" (Matthew 22:39). In Luke 10:29, a man asks Jesus, "Who is my neighbor?" Jesus answers by telling the story of the Good Samaritan. This man takes pity on a man who has been beaten and robbed. The Samaritan bandages the man's wounds, takes him to an inn where he can be cared for, and pays for his treatment. Jesus points to the Good Samaritan as someone loving his neighbor by being merciful to someone in need.

What does a modern-day Good Samaritan look like?

She has many faces, but one was a young girl in Kenya who loved to run fast and run far. Jacqueline Kiplimo believed that she could become a world-class runner and earn money to help feed her many younger siblings. The opportunity came to enter a marathon race in China, and she believed she could win the ten-thousand-dollar first prize.

Jacqueline was leading the women's division when a male runner arrived at the water station at the ten-kilometer mark. The man was running at a good pace but had trouble staying hydrated because a birth defect had left him without hands, and he struggled to drink from the slippery plastic bottles. The rules were that fans or race officials could not assist him or else he would be disqualified. But Jacqueline saw that he needed help. She grabbed a water bottle and tipped it up to his mouth to help him get the fluid his body needed to keep running the race. Then she ran at his pace with the bottle and helped him sip while they ran.

As runners passed Jacqueline, the lifelong dreams of money to help her family ran by with them. This modern-day Good Samaritan stayed with the man in need until they were just four kilometers from the finish line. When she was certain he could finish the race, she sped up and, astonishingly, finished second! When asked how she felt about losing the big prize because she'd slowed down to help a fellow athlete, she said, "Money isn't everything."

When Jacqueline returned home to Kenya, she couldn't offer her younger siblings much money, but she gave them something more valuable. She demonstrated that loving is more important than winning.[6]

Jacqueline inspires me. I'm not running a marathon, but who runs past me every day on the track where I walk my golden retriever, Cali? She may have both her hands and be able to hold her water bottle, but do I see the pain in her eyes? Am I looking? Or am I so intent on my own schedule, my own life, and my own pain and needs that I walk right by and don't see? Oh, my friend, may we see and love like Jacqueline!

The Elephant Herd Loves One Another

A women's Bible study group in Texas meets with the goal of loving one another. They call themselves the Elephant Herd. When I heard that, I thought, *Why would anyone want to be in a group associated with huge, wrinkled, lumbering animals? Why didn't they name their group something more feminine and colorful, like the Peacock Pack or the Butterfly Beauties?* But when I talked to the leader of the group, she just smiled and began to tell me about female elephants.

Elephants are one of the most empathetic species on earth. Female elephants are pregnant for two years. (Yes, two years, the longest pregnancy of any living mammal. Let's give a shout-out to female elephants everywhere!)

In the wild, when a mama elephant gives birth, the other females in the herd back their four-ton hulky bodies into a circle around Mama to protect her. They close ranks. They stomp and kick up soil to ward off predators looking for a baby elephant for dinner.

If an enemy approaches, they trumpet and stomp a warning: *If you want to attack my friend while she's vulnerable, you'll have to get through forty tons of female aggression first.*

After the baby elephant is born, the sister elephants do two things: They kick sand or dirt over the newborn to protect its fragile skin from the sun, and then they trumpet again, this time as a symphony of celebration, of sisterhood, celebrating together something beautiful being born in a harsh, wild world.

Like their animal counterpart, the Elephant Herd ladies actively love one another. They share lunches together. They share the good and the hard times and hold one another accountable.

How do they support each other? Once, they set their alarms for 5:10 a.m. and prayed daily for one woman who wanted to quit smoking. They spent six years praying for two sons and rejoiced together when they saw God work in both their lives. Love shows up. And the practice of letting ourselves be loved is the only way to survive our hardest seasons.

But what do you do when you're the one in pain? Can you be a Good Samaritan to others? Perhaps not when your pain is raw and bleeding, but maybe you can reach out to others when a measure of healing has taken place. God began to bring women to me when the scabs on my heart were still very tender. What miraculous joy filled my soul as I prayed over Patsy, whose daughter had cancer. My pain was able to connect with her pain. Healing occurred in that moment. Mom to mom, we wept and sought God's wisdom and peace together.

My Friends Love Me

Women often tell me, "I don't know what to say or do when someone is in pain or suffering. I just feel awkward." I think we make it hard when love can be a simple "I'm sorry for your pain." My friend Nancy did this for me.

Years ago, I was in my kitchen in Vienna, Austria, weeping because I didn't know how to love a mixed-up teen. My doorbell rang. I thought, *Oh no, I don't want to see or talk to anyone.* My nose was running, my eyes were red, and I was a wreck. The door opened, and my friend Nancy walked in, hugged me, and said, "Linda, I'm not here to talk. I'm going in your living room to pray for you and your teenager. I'll get up and leave quietly. Pretend I'm not here." How could I pretend she wasn't there? Now I was in my kitchen weeping because the arms of love were so kind and so sensitive.

Love can also be words on sticky notes.

My daughter Robin, who was recovering from cancer, flew from New Jersey to Arizona to be with my other daughter, Joy, at a cancer-treatment center. I flew in from Colorado to join them. Our days were a combination of delight and sadness—delight to be with my adult daughters and sadness witnessing Joy's intense suffering. The doctors had few answers. Robin and I sat with Joy, sharing memories of years in Vienna, until Joy slept.

When I returned home a few days later, I put my suitcase down and looked at my kitchen counter. Little angels named Lorraine and Valerie had been here. Multiple vases of bright, cheerful flowers decorated my kitchen counter. My fridge had been cleaned and filled with food. But the most special treat was the scores of Post-it notes hidden everywhere—in my pantry, in my cupboards, in my desk. Each note contained a message of hope.

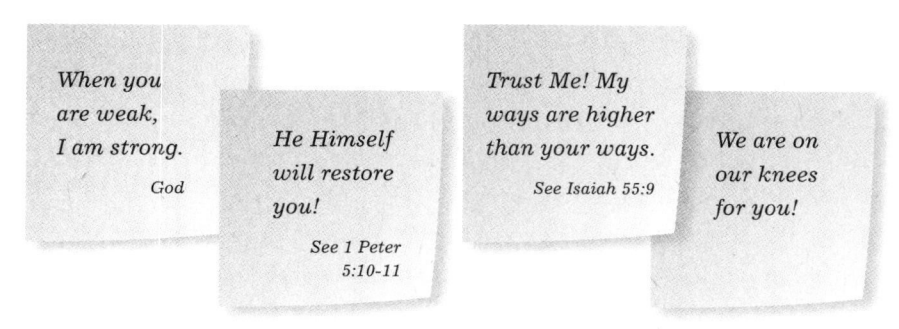

> *When you are weak, I am strong.*
> God

> *He Himself will restore you!*
> See 1 Peter 5:10-11

> *Trust Me! My ways are higher than your ways.*
> See Isaiah 55:9

> *We are on our knees for you!*

Even three months later, I found a yellow note on a jar of parsley that said, "Don't panic. I've got this! – God." Who knew love came on sticky notes?

The love of Lorraine and Valerie so touched my heart. They don't know that all their handwritten sticky notes are saved in a Ziploc bag. Who saves sticky notes? I do when they have messages from God wrapped in the love of friends.

Reach out your arms and receive God's love for you. May you feel a warm embrace from the Father who loves you, from friends who care, and perhaps even in unusual ways, like sticky notes in your pantry.

God's agapē love is here to carry you when life hurts. Let the love of God saturate your heart. Yes, looking at the loss in our lives is still hard. We avoid it. We don't want to think about it—or deal with it. Only when we receive and experience the love of God can we find the strength to go down into loss, to really see our losses and accept them, and to move forward. My friend, I promise that you'll be glad you looked at loss in a new way.

Heart Skill
A PLAN

Create your own spiritual workout plan that will help you grow in loving God with all your heart, soul, mind, and strength. Review the plans of Linda, Alix, and Kim and Tracy for ideas.

CHAPTER 3

LOSS

*It is how we respond to loss that matters.
That response will largely determine the quality,
the direction, and the impact of our lives.*
JERRY SITTSER

Loss

We started this book with hope because hope is what is lost, and we want to move toward it. Then we talked about love because it's God's love that fills us with hope and enables us to bless others, even in our pain.

Hope and *love* are words that make us smile. But *loss*? Not so much. Still, if we are to receive what Got wants to say to us during hard times, we must look at loss.

One phone call from the doctor can change the course of our lives. One harsh conversation with a loved one, and your world can collapse. For me, all it took was one misstep in the wrong direction, and my future was forever altered.

I grabbed my bag with my boarding pass and passport and followed the line of people snaking toward the plane. I was on my way to speak at an Intimate Issues conference[1] in Ireland with Lorraine, my soul sister, where a sold-out crowd of women from all over the country were gathering to spend ten hours learning about intimacy with their husbands and with God. Lorraine was already in Dublin with a team of eight women who had come to serve in various capacities. I was excited to join them.

I took a few steps down the staircase toward the boarding area. That's the last thing I remember.

Jody called Lorraine to give her the bad news.

"I'm so sorry, but Linda's not coming. Linda fell down a flight of stairs and landed on her head. She has bleeding on the brain. She's suffered a traumatic brain injury and is in a trauma hospital."

I called out from my hospital bed in the background. "I'm coming, Lorraine! I'm coming to Ireland."

After Jody hung up the phone he chuckled. "Honey, even when you're not fully conscious you're telling everyone what you're going to do." Jody was right. I was an "in-charge gal," but, oh, I felt so out of control as I touched the stitches on my face. My injuries were severe. I couldn't will myself to Ireland, no matter how much I wanted to.

I thought surely my strength would return soon, but that's not what happened. Brains don't heal like broken arms. The doctor doesn't put a cast on and say, "In eight weeks we'll take this off and your brain will be good as new." God, the Master Craftsman, designed every brain to heal in its own way and own time.

Mine seemed to heal very slowly. I began canceling all events for the upcoming year.

Certain losses with my brain injury were immediate. God gave me a quick brain that made razor-fast decisions. *Multitask* was my middle name. All that was gone. Now I processed in slow motion. Focusing on anything seemed impossible. My memory was gappy, and recalling names or numbers felt hopeless. Noise and light caused problems, and I could no longer drive at night.

Other losses unfolded over time. About eighteen months after my traumatic brain injury (TBI), I went to an evening of worship with two friends. The worship leader asked if anyone needed healing. People around the auditorium raised their hands. My friends raised my arms and then laid hands on me and prayed for my healing. But God whispered something very different to my heart. It was so clear that I couldn't miss it: *Linda, I want you weak.*

I love it when God speaks clearly. No doubts. It is Him, His message to me. But this wasn't exactly what I was hoping for. God wanted me weak? Oh, I knew my Bible. Paul said he took pleasure in his weakness because his thorn in the flesh caused him to exchange self-dependence for God-dependence. He wrote that God's grace was all you needed, that God's power worked best in weakness (see 2 Corinthians 12:9). I wanted God to be strong in me. But did I really have to be weak for that to happen?

Let's be honest. We all like strong better than weak. We want to be strong in body, strong in brain, strong emotionally and spiritually, strong everything! None of us choose to be weak.

But it was what God had chosen for me. Weakness came to live with me, to be my companion 24/7. We had a conversation. It went down something like this.

Weakness: Hello, Linda. My name is Weakness. You are no longer in charge. From now on, I am in charge. This will mean changes for you.

Me: What kinds of changes?

Weakness: For starters, there will be changes in your body. Your feet will go numb. You will get neuropathy, which means you won't be able to feel when you walk or stand. No more high heels for you. You'll also have to stop wearing those open-toed sandals you love because your feet will turn blue.

Me: Well, I do love those sandals, but that's not the end of the world. I can deal with that.

Weakness: Good. You'll also suffer from adult-onset ADHD. And you'll experience unexpected seizures in which you'll black out and fall.

Me: Really? You mean no matter what medication I take, how well I eat, or how many brain exercises I do, I'll never get completely better?

Weakness: Correct. But you will find coping skills. God will still use you, and you will still be effective for Him.

Me: How is that possible if my body isn't working like it should?

Weakness: Ah, that's the beauty of it. Although your body and your brain will have some limitations, there's no limit to what your spirit can do. In fact, the limitations in your body will push you toward greater dependence upon God. Your brokenness will display His glory, and He will delight in you. You will love Him and serve Him in ways you never dreamed possible.

My friend, as I share my losses with you, I wonder, what are your losses? Have you lost a marriage? A job? A home? Your health? Has someone close to you died? Or betrayed you? Or violated you? Have you lost your reputation? Your motivation? Your inspiration? Losses come in all shapes and sizes, but they all have one thing in common: All loss causes pain.

In this chapter, I want us to consider how we think about our loss and the pain associated with it. I have learned to ask myself two basic questions:

1. Do I accept my loss?
2. How does God use loss to change me?

How we answer these questions exposes our attitude about our loss and reveals whether we are stuck in our pain or moving gracefully through it.

Do I Accept My Loss?

Cathy was a Christian therapist when, in her early thirties, she suffered a severe stroke while eight months pregnant with her second child. This led to brain surgery and a C-section. Cathy had to relearn walking and talking. She did all this as a single mom because her Christian husband had walked out on her just before her stroke. So much loss for one person!

Over time, Cathy began to heal, to walk and talk again, but her mental processing was so slow that she could not continue her job as a therapist. After working many different jobs, this brave woman went to massage school and became a massage therapist.

I went to Cathy so she could massage the rocks out of my shoulders. We developed a special friendship as we swapped stories about the challenges of living with a brain injury. One morning as I lay face down on her massage table, she asked me a question that rocked my world.

"Linda, have you accepted that you are not the same person you were before your injury?"

I glibly said yes and then cried all the way home. Had I? Had I really come to grips with the fact that this loss had changed me? That I would never again be who I was before my fall? I looked the same, but I felt very different on the inside.

The first step in dealing with any loss is to accept it, to stop stuffing the grief that threatens to surface, to simply let it come. How do we do that?

> ~ *Grieve the loss.* Cathy said that the emotions attached to her loss came in waves. Sometimes a wave forcefully knocked her down and pulled her under; other times, it gently washed over her. Either way, the wave shaped her, just as

the waves in the ocean shape the shore. Both Cathy and I had to keep telling ourselves that whether the emotions were forceful or gentle, bold or subtle, we should embrace them as a normal part of loss.

What I've learned about the grief waves is this: If you resist, they persist. But if you feel, they help you heal. Our bodies were meant to process grief, not to store it. So open wide your heart and let the emotions do their work in you. And in this process, remember to be oh-so-gentle with yourself. Grief is exhausting. Give yourself grace . . . and all the time you need.

~ *Accept the scope of the loss.* Cathy's losses affected not only her but also her children (since she could no longer care for all their needs), her mother (who came to live with Cathy for seven months after the surgeries), and her coworkers and clients (Cathy had to leave her job as a therapist). Who is affected by your loss? Make a list. It's important to acknowledge that part of your grief is the sadness you feel on behalf of others who also suffer because of your loss.

~ *Redefine yourself in light of your loss.* Cathy's loss meant changing her title. She had to strike through the letters *LPC* after her name and add two *d* labels that she never wanted as part of her identity—*divorced* and *disabled*.

I'll never forget the first time I said "I am handicapped" out loud. Saying this gave me boldness to make my label even more specific: "I have a traumatic brain injury." "I have seizures. I have epilepsy." Last year I taught counselors at a large church how to tenderly encourage someone with my challenges. It was such a joy to see my pain be used to encourage others. Pain redeemed is better than pain removed. God will use anything we lay before Him for His glory.

Does your loss cause you to have a new label? Maybe the label is *widow*. Maybe it's a job title you don't want. Or a classification you never desired. Or maybe it's adjusting to the changes that come with a new season of life, like kids entering school or going away to school, the empty nest, or retirement. Coming to terms with your current situation will free you to move forward in your loss.

Maybe you're saying, *Linda, I've done all these things. I've grieved my loss, I've accepted the scope of it, and I've come to grips with how it's shaped my identity. But I still don't know what to do with this huge ball of pain.*

Well, I have good news for you. No, great news! God's Word has an answer for what to do with your pain. But the bad news? You may not like that answer. I sure didn't like it when Weakness told me it was going to be my constant companion. But remember, Weakness also promised what I really wanted most: that my loss would push me to greater dependence on God and that, in my brokenness, I would delight God and bring glory to Him.

Before I tell you what God's Word says you are to do with your pain, my friend, let me speculate about a few things you want.

I'm thinking that you want to be more like Jesus.

I think you're sick and tired of your subtle and blatant character flaws and you want them gone.

I imagine you want to be known by your family and friends as a woman of faith who is a rock of wisdom.

I'm guessing all this is true, or you wouldn't still be reading this book.

But let me ask you this: Are you willing to let pain be the transforming agent that God uses to shape your character?

How Does God Use Loss to Change Me?

People ask me often, "Can't God change me in the good times?" Yes. But I've come to see that God meets me in a particularly tender and holy way when I've been down in the trenches, down in a deep, dark place. In the pain, He has given me Himself, and He gently (and sometimes not so gently) molds my character. I am convinced that certain character traits can only be birthed from the womb of loss.

God's Word confirms this. Get ready, because I want to show you the toughest verse in the Bible, my favorite love-hate word in the Bible, and the fattest promise in the Bible, all of which are found in the first four verses of James.[2]

The Toughest Verse in the Bible

Bob Sorge is known as "the speaker who can't talk" because of a physician error during a surgery over thirty years ago that reduced his voice to a whisper. Sorge, who has personally experienced deep pain and loss—he was a pastor at the time of his surgery—calls James 1:2 the "toughest verse in the Bible."[3] Let's look at a few different translations of this verse so we can better understand its meaning:

> Consider it wholly joyful, my brethren, whenever you are enveloped in or encounter trials of any sort or fall into various temptations.
> JAMES 1:2, AMPC

> Consider it a sheer gift, friends, when tests and challenges come at you from all sides.
> JAMES 1:2, MSG

> When all kinds of trials and temptations crowd into your lives . . . don't resent them as intruders, but welcome them as friends!
> JAMES 1:2, PHILLIPS

What? How can this be? James is saying that when you lose your job, when your home is destroyed by fire, when your husband walks out the door into the arms of another woman, when your child is deathly ill—you should be joyful? How can James say that trials, pain, and loss are opportunities for great joy?

This doesn't make sense. Most of us find joy when we escape trials! Pain as a friend? A gift? How is this even possible? The pathway is found in the next two verses.

My Favorite Love-Hate Word in the Bible

After James's shocking statement, he adds this:

> Be assured and understand that the trial and proving of your faith bring out endurance and steadfastness and patience.
>
> But let endurance and steadfastness and patience have full play and do a thorough work, so that you may be [people] perfectly and fully developed [with no defects], lacking in nothing.
> JAMES 1:3-4, AMPC

James is saying that "when your faith is tested, your endurance has a chance to grow" (James 1:3, NLT). To *endure* means that you press on, plug along, slog along. It means "to persist with clenched fists," "to not relent even when spent." The word implies sweating, grunting, groaning, and—can I just say it?—pain. Does that sound fun to you? Me neither.

That's why *endurance* is my love-hate word. The flesh part of me hates endurance, but the spirit part of me loves it—because only through endurance are the deepest longings of my heart accomplished. Sorge says it beautifully:

> When you stay in faith in the midst of a painful trial, you are releasing the most powerful forces imaginable in the kingdom of God. Endurance . . . is so life-changing that it has the ability to do in you what nothing else can do.[4]

Sorge knows the power of endurance. James also knew its power. This is why he could be joyful *in* the trial (not *for* the trial)—because James saw beyond the trial.

The Fattest Promise in the Bible

> Let the process go on until that endurance is fully developed, and you will find you have become [people] of mature character.
>
> JAMES 1:4, PHILLIPS

I dare you to find a stronger promise in the Bible than James 1:4. When you endure in faith, you release forces that have the power to transform everything about you. It is possible to be so transformed that you emerge from the trial as a woman of mature character.

What? Weak, broken, brain-damaged me? As I endure, I can

become mature? Complete? Lacking nothing? What does this mean practically? Paul describes the maturity of a Christ follower as someone who has the fruit of the Spirit: love, joy, peace, patience, kindness, goodness, faithfulness, gentleness, and self-control (Galatians 5:22-23). What fruit of the Spirit is God producing in you as you endure in your loss?

James goes on to tell us that while we are fighting through our trials, as we are maturing, the generous God of wisdom breathes His wisdom into us so we can keep on keeping on. All we have to do is ask, and He will pour wisdom into us. Look with me at this great promise:

> If any of you is deficient in wisdom, let him ask of the giving God [Who gives] to everyone liberally and ungrudgingly, without reproaching or faultfinding, and it will be given him.
> JAMES 1:5, AMPC

Can you see how far we've come in just a few short verses? We started with trials, loss, pain. But we are told that as we endure with faith, a power is released in us to transform us, to make us mature, full of wisdom, and covered in grace. But wait, there's more:

> God blesses those who patiently endure testing and temptation. Afterward they will receive the crown of life that God has promised to those who love him.
> JAMES 1:12, NLT

Could we ask for more? Untold blessings from God? The crown of life? Is James talking about a real crown? Yes. At the end of our lives, when we meet our Lord face-to-face, if we endure, we won't be empty-handed. We'll have a crown to cast in praise and honor at the feet of our blessed Lord! I want that crown, don't you? But it seems that this crown is not only a reward in eternity but also a reward in the present. According to Zane Hodges,

> The crown of life is received in heaven but also refers to . . . the enrichment of our *temporal* experience of *life* . . . that James has in mind. . . . Life will be richer, deeper, fuller for his Christian readers if they are among those who . . . reach the end of their trials victoriously. Indeed, every time we successfully endure a period of trouble, *the crown of life* will be awarded to us anew.[5]

I love the heart of James, Jesus' half brother, who is said to have been known as Camel Knees because his knees were hard and black from kneeling in prayer so often for his people.[6] He wrote hard truths to encourage all of us to endure. *Oh, blessed Word, work Your power in me and in each one of us so we might be wise and be given the crown of life!*

Endurance Hall of Fame

You've probably read the "Faith Hall of Fame" in Hebrews 11, which lists men and women of the Bible who trusted God. I think we also need an "Endurance Hall of Fame"—a list of those who remained faithful to God despite enduring incredible loss and pain. I'd include Paul, Job, Joseph, Mary, Esther, Habakkuk, and many others on my list. Who would be on your list? Here's a list of contemporaries who have inspired me. As you read, I urge you to consider your own list of people who inspire you to endure even when life is hard.

Cathy Deschaine

You met Cathy earlier in this chapter, when she was massaging rocks out of my shoulders. She suffered a major stroke and endured indescribable challenges as a single mom. She almost gave up, but in the end, she endured. She fought for her kids, her faith, her health. She also fought to regain the *LPC* credentials behind her name. It took fifteen years, but she is once again working as a therapist, now with broader experience and greater skill to help others in pain. I shout, "Hurrah for Cathy!"

Dr. Daniel Wallace

I know about Daniel Wallace because my husband uses his 860-page textbook, *Greek Grammar beyond the Basics*, every morning when he reads the New Testament in Greek. At the time the book was published, Dr. Dan was fluent in six languages: English, Greek, Hebrew, Latin, French, and German. A year after Dan wrote his Greek tome, he contracted encephalitis. An article about Dan's devastating health journey from *Voice: Dallas Theological Seminary Magazine* explains: "Dan spent nearly a year in a wheelchair and . . . was unable to focus on any studies for more than a few minutes a day. For several months, he slept twenty-two hours each day. He lost his memory of basic things. . . . His knowledge of French, German, and Latin disappeared, and his understanding of Hebrew and Greek reverted to beginner-level."[7]

Many would have just given up, but Dr. Dan endured. "I had to relearn Greek," he said. "I taught myself Greek using the textbook that I myself had published the year before!" He added, "Over five decades wrestling with the Greek New Testament has been for me an act of worship."[8]

I learn from Dr. Dan that endurance can also become worship. His faithful endurance encourages me to press on.

Joni Eareckson Tada

At age seventeen, Joni Eareckson Tada suffered a diving accident that left her paralyzed from the neck down. At times she felt hopeless, even to the point of wanting to die, but she pressed through her pain and used her brain and limited body function to become a world-renowned speaker, writer, and artist (she paints with a mouth brush). Joni says,

> In a way, I hope I can bring my wheelchair to heaven. I know that's not theologically correct, but I hope I can wheel it up to Jesus, hold his nail-pierced hands, and say, "Jesus, see this wheelchair? You were right when you said that in this world we would have trouble. This wheelchair was a lot of trouble. But the weaker I was in it, the harder I leaned on you. And the harder I leaned on you, the stronger I discovered you to be. Thank you for giving me this bruising of a blessing. My wheelchair showed me a side of your grace that I never would have seen otherwise."[9]

The response of Joni, Dan, Cathy, and many others inspires me to press through my pain and endure in faith. As author Jerry Sittser writes, "It is not . . . the *experience* of loss that becomes the defining moment of our lives, for that is as inevitable as death. . . . It is how we *respond* to loss that matters. That response will largely determine the quality, the direction, and the impact of our lives."[10]

My Endurance Marathon

For eighteen months, like Camel Knees James, I'd fallen to my knees over and over, pouring out prayers to my gracious Father.

On this particular day, my daughter Robin was in the hospital alone. "Oh Holy One," I cried, "comfort Robin as she suffers through her body rejecting the chemo. Her blood levels are tanking; she's close to death. The doctors have no answers."

God answered my prayer for Robin. But it took many months for her blood levels to crawl back to anywhere near normal.

Then came the call from Joy and her cancer diagnosis. *Really, God? Two daughters with cancer?* The ball of pain inside me felt like it was about to explode. I didn't know I could hurt this much. But I knew where to go: to my knees . . . again.

> *Oh, Lord, I trust You. Heal my Joy. Let her live for her husband, Steven; for her daughter, Annika; and for all of us who love her. I look to You, my faithful God. Oh, Gracious One, do a miracle. Please heal Joy. Please, Abba, give life to my daughter. I entrust her to Your loving arms.*

In every loss, I knew God my Father had heard my constant cries. I would wait for His answer.

Heart Skill
A JOURNAL

Keep a Thankful Journal. This journal will help you maintain a balanced perspective between what you suffer and the blessings that surround you. For the next week, write at least three to five things a day for which you are thankful.

CHAPTER 4

LAMENT

Lament is a prayer in pain that leads to trust.
MARK VROEGOP

Lament

LAMENT

Annika's Lament

I've learned what it feels like to cry so much your eyes become dry and the skin around them starts to peel.

I know what it looks like to slowly die—I know what a last breath sounds like.

I know what it feels like to lose your balance at the sight of death, to sit in a corner and wait for the prayer to end.

I know what cries of pure sadness sound like and what a parent's eyes look like when they've lost a daughter.

I know what love looks like, surrounding you as you leave.[1]

ANNIKA DUPUIS (JOY'S DAUGHTER, AGE TWENTY-THREE)

My granddaughter Annika found poetic words to express her grief as she watched her mother's life—my daughter Joy's life—leave her body. Me? I struggled to find words. As one author says,

> The greatest loss is that of a child. There are no words to describe that loss. If you've lost your spouse, you're a widow or widower. If you've lost both parents, you're an orphan. But to lose a child, there is no descriptive word. The grief and pain are wordless.[2]

I said that there were no words for my deep sorrow, but I was wrong. There is a word—I just didn't know it, nor did I realize the profound comfort and encouragement this word would bring. The word is *lament*.

What do you think when you hear the word *lament*? Does it sound depressing? Maybe it conjures up images trapped in dusty, ancient Scriptures of people wailing and pounding their chests in sorrow?

What is lament? In the simplest of terms, lament, as seen in the Bible, is passionate expression of sorrow. My personal amplified definition of *lament* is "to groan in prayer and wail out sorrow before God to expel the ball of pain inside me."

But I've learned that lament is so much more. In his book *A Sacred Sorrow*, Michael Card taught me that lament is worship in a minor key. Mark Vroegop, in *Dark Clouds, Deep Mercy*, showed me that "lament is a prayer in pain that leads to trust."[3] David, in the Psalms, showed an intimate oneness with God as he lamented his pain. I read the words of these men and I say yes: yes to worship, yes to trust, yes to intimacy! If lamenting can offer all this, then I say yes to lament—even if pain is a part of it.

Oh, friend, as you experience pain and long for hope, lament can be a powerful, sweet gift to you, as it has been for me. Vroegop says lament is the following:

~ "*It is a language for loss*. Lament is the historic prayer language for hurting Christians."
~ "*It is the solution for silence*. Lament cracks the door open to talk to God again—even if it's messy."
~ "*It is a framework for feelings*. Lament endorses expression, but only the kind with the right objective."
~ "*It is a process for our pain*. Lament is more than something that comes out of you. It is part of the process happening in you."[4]

The book *Dark Clouds, Deep Mercy* was so important to me that Jody and I suggested we study it with our small group from church. The five couples who gathered in our living room to talk about the book were unusual—three of the men had been seminary professors; the other two men were leaders of international mission organizations. And all five of the women were amazing in unique ways. It's safe to say that the people in the room were well versed in all things Christian and biblical. Mark, a warm-hearted lover of people who'd been a seminary professor for nineteen years, said, "I'm so grateful you chose this book. It made me realize I know nothing about lament."

If a seminary professor knows nothing, where does that leave the rest of us? The Bible talks extensively about lament. One third of the Psalms are called lament songs. One book of the Bible, Lamentations, is devoted specifically to the idea of lament. The books of Job and Jeremiah are filled with the language of lament. Why do so many of us lack understanding of a subject that the Bible talks so much about?

The Disappearance of Lament

Timothy Keller, in his excellent book *Walking with God through Pain and Suffering*, discusses how lament disappeared from the mind and heart of the modern Christian in America. I didn't know that happened; did you? But Keller says that after the Reformation, the early Reformers created a culture in which the expression of doubts or complaints against God was frowned upon. Christians were taught not to weep or cry but to show God their faith through unflinching, joyful acceptance of His will. This went so far that some early Lutheran writers were concerned that the book of Job was even included in the Bible, since questioning God—as Job did—was such a terrible sin.[5]

Of course, people today in the twenty-first century don't realize that our ancestors, wanting to do right, got things very wrong. We don't realize how intricately threads of stoicism were woven into the fabric of our American culture. Lorraine explains how this was true for her:

> I was seven years old when the plane my father was flying crashed into a mountain bluff and killed him and his brother. At the funeral, people cried, but after that, life went on as usual. No one talked about my dad, and I wasn't encouraged to talk about him either. One day I was sitting on our front porch steps feeling very sad, and a boy in our neighborhood started chanting, "Crybaby, crybaby." As I grew older, I watched adults around me paste smiles on their faces and say "I'm fine" when I knew they weren't. In our family, crying or showing deep sorrow was considered a sign of weakness.

Our Western culture has no collective framework to process pain. A biblical scholar said that after the horrific attack on 9/11, the American church had no songs to sing.[6] Contrast this with the Hebrew rabbis in Israel who had laments to sing after the October 7, 2023, massacre of 1,200 people by Hamas. Because lament has provided a framework for their grief for centuries, a plethora of songs, prayers, and rituals exist in their culture. In fact, if a Jewish child dies, the parents observe four stages of grief. *Aninut* is pre-burial mourning. *Shiva* is a seven-day period following the burial. *Shloshim* is a thirty-day mourning period. And finally *yahrzeit* marks the one-year anniversary date.

What do we do in our church when someone dies? We hold a memorial service, and the next day, everyone goes back to work! No wonder we don't know what to do with our grief.

My friend Casey grew up in a strong Christian home where both parents were leaders in the church. When Casey learned that her husband had become addicted to porn and was seeking sex from prostitutes, she didn't know what to do with her shock, sorrow, and outrage. She did what she was raised to do—she read Scripture, quoted Scripture, worshiped, and prayed—but nothing eased her intense pain. Finally, out of desperation, she went to a wise Christian counselor who told her, "Casey, you need to be raw and real with your emotions. After all, Jesus was a 'man of sorrows'—a man acquainted with grief. He wept and expressed strong emotion." The counselor's words unlocked something in Casey's heart and gave her permission to lament. Casey shares,

> The next morning, I went to a private place where I was able to weep and wail before the Lord, to shout and beg until so much gunk was running out both my eyes and nose that I couldn't see or breathe. I was glad no one could see me, dripping and drained of all emotion, lying in a fetal position on the floor. But ah, it was good. I felt cleansed inside.

Aren't you glad that we have a Savior who felt things deeply and honestly expressed His grief? He wept over the death of Lazarus. He shed anguished tears over the sins of Jerusalem. He wailed in agony, so much so that He sweat blood as He begged His Abba for a different plan than the one that required horrific suffering on the cross.

While Lorraine and I have been writing this chapter, we've

been on our knees worshiping together with Matt Redman singing the holy worship song "Son of Suffering."[7] Aren't you glad we have a God who weeps and bleeds for us? A God who feels deeply? We have a God who not only hears our anguish but knows what it is to suffer Himself.

God feels your pain; you do not suffer alone. As you weep, God weeps with you.

The Journey of Lament

Left alone, the pain-ball inside us can quickly turn toxic—leaking out bitterness, fear, and isolation and changing who we are. But God offers us a surprising and beautiful way to process the pain, a path toward becoming more healed on the other side: the honest, gut-deep practice of lament.

Asaph, the author of Psalm 77, has been a teacher in helping me understand the process of lament. God has used this beautiful psalm to show me the journey of lament:

- ~ Cry out your complaint.
- ~ Choose to remember.

Cry Out Your Complaint

While we see the reality of lament throughout the Psalms, the psalmist Asaph in Psalm 77 shows us how even the most profound and painful emotion is welcome before God. Why do I say "welcome"? Because the God who inspired Scripture wanted us to see this picture of relating to Him in loss.

Asaph begins Psalm 77 by saying he will seek the Lord in his day of trouble. But as he thinks about God, he falls into a pit of despair. He's not merely sad—his brain and body are so despondent that, if he were living today, he'd probably be hospitalized for clinical depression. He says that even thinking about God causes him deep anguish:

> My soul refused to be comforted.
> When I remember God, then I am disturbed. . . .
> You have held my eyelids open;
> I am so troubled that I cannot speak.
> PSALM 77:2-4, NASB

Have you ever been in so much pain that you couldn't speak? So deeply troubled that sleep refused to come? Asaph's soul is infused with disbelief, doubts, and accusations. This painful place leads him to ask six rhetorical questions:

> Has the Lord rejected me forever?
>   Will he never again be kind to me?
> Is his unfailing love gone forever?
>   Have his promises permanently failed?
> Has God forgotten to be gracious?
>   Has he slammed the door on his compassion?
> PSALM 77:7-9, NLT

Are you surprised that these harsh, accusing questions directed at God are in the Bible? My Bible tells me to always be full of thanksgiving—to not gripe, complain, nag, or vent. Your Bible says the same thing. But your Bible (and mine as well) also gives us permission to honestly express our doubts, struggles, and complaints.

Finally, after honestly asking God all his hard, hard questions, Asaph reveals in verse 10 the deepest pain in his heart: "It is my grief, that the right hand of the Most High has changed" (Psalm 77:10, NASB).

This is what really tears him apart. This raw accusation is the basis for all his other complaints. He is saying, *You, God, have changed. Not just what You failed to give that You said You'd give—Your loving-kindness, Your promises, Your compassion—but Y-O-U, the Most High, have changed.*[8]

What could be more painful than having the One you trusted—the One in whom you placed all your hopes, the One you counted on being there no matter what—turn out to be someone different than you knew Him to be?

Asaph holds nothing back. He expresses it all.

From this dear psalmist I'm encouraged to do these things:

~ Pray my struggles.
~ Pray my questions.
~ Be real! Be raw! Be honest before God!

For Asaph, crying out to God was an act of faith. Praying his struggles was an act of faith. Praying his questions was an act of faith. And so, longing for that kind of faith in my own pain, I wrote my own lament of honest questions:

God, do You see me in my pain?
Why didn't I get cancer instead of my daughters?
Where are You, God?
If You love me and my family, why is this happening?
God, will You help me trust You, even in my pain?

My lament is messy. It's not well written. It doesn't rhyme; there's nothing lovely about it. Yet it is an act of faith to be honest and raw before God, and I think He sees that as lovely. I came to believe that prayerful lament—even if it is messy—is better than silence.

You may feel that lament seems too honest, too risky, too open, too everything. You may feel that airing your complaints would be disrespectful to God or show a lack of trust in Him. But, my dear friend, expressing your angst can unravel the pain-ball inside. I promise you that it is better than giving God the silent treatment. What do you think your silence says to your God? Bringing your whole self—even and maybe especially your pain—keeps the channels of communication open between you and God. It will keep you in relationship when pain and loss make you want to shut down.

Choose to Remember

Maybe Asaph's words and my words sound like complaining to you, but "pray-complaining" is connection with God. And what we see from Asaph is that his persistence in staying before God changed his pray-complaining to *I-will* praying. In lament, we express the sorrow we feel, but we also rehearse the truths we believe.[9] We choose to remember—and as we do, we find ourselves and our focus changing.

In verses 11 and 12, a dramatic shift takes place in Asaph's heart. Asaph turns his eyes away from his gloom and puts them on his God. This choice takes him from hopeless to hopeful. It's like his heart is on a hinge, swinging to a different place as he voices three specific *I will remember*s:

> *I will remember* the deeds of the LORD.
> *I will remember* Your wonders of old.
> *I will remember* Your work and meditate on Your mighty deeds.
> BASED ON PSALM 77:11-12, ESV

Asaph's remembering ushers him out of unbelief and into the presence of God. I believe that certain measures of God's presence are only revealed in the depths of mourning. I imagine God enveloping Asaph and comforting him as he remembers. "Blessed are those who mourn, for they shall be comforted" (Matthew 5:4, NASB).

Through my journey of lament during the cancer years with my daughters, I also experienced God's comfort in my remembering. Instead of focusing on all that cancer had stolen, I grabbed my will by the scruff of the neck and told myself to search for beauty in the midst of my sorrow. *Remember,* I said. *Remember the beauty in the ashes and don't stop looking until you find it.*

> *Oh, God, I remember the day Robin rang the bell to mark the end of her prescribed chemo treatments. Tears ran down my face as I watched the video over and over—Robin ringing the bell, hospital staff and fellow sufferers clapping and cheering. I praise You, Father, for sparing her life. I thank You for slowly healing her broken body.*
>
> *Lord, I remember the day Joy breathed her last breath. A mom and dad shouldn't have to watch their daughter die. It's the wrong order. I remember that the day was filled with songs, prayers, and sharing by all the family and many friends. Love filled the space in the room around her bed as Annika and Robin took turns lying beside Joy and stroking her hair. After Joy breathed her last breath, Steven, Joy's husband, hugged Jody and me and said, "This has been a beautiful day."*
>
> *Gracious God, I am grateful for tangible symbols of remembrance. Steven and Annika purchased a park bench with Joy's name on it and placed it by her favorite hiking trail in Santa Barbara. Our family and friends can go there anytime to reflect*

upon her life. Lorraine planted a "Joy tree" in her front yard with a memorial plaque. I'm at her place often, and when I see the tree, I remember my beloved daughter, and I'm grateful that You gave me so many precious years with her.

Holy One, I remember Your arms holding me as my heart broke in pieces. As I reflect on the cancer years, I see that You were with me. You held me. You, Abba, constantly gave me Your strength. Your Word was a light to guide my feet. I thank You, God, for Your Word, Your presence, and Your voice—three blessed gifts. I remember. I bow. I worship. Your presence sustains me.

Sometimes, Lord, it's hard to remember Your blessings in the middle of pain—but I remember, and I thank You.

Do I have answers as to why Joy died so suddenly, just a few months after her diagnosis? Can I explain why Robin has suffered so terribly? No. Sometimes no satisfactory answers exist for the painful questions we ask. But remembering turns my eyes away from my pain and causes me to look upon my mighty God. And like Asaph, I have found that remembering God's deeds, wonders, and works causes my heart to worship. Listen to Asaph's worship:

> O God, your ways are holy.
> Is there any god as mighty as you?
> You are the God of great wonders!
> You demonstrate your awesome power among
> the nations.
>
> PSALM 77:13-14, NLT

If Asaph were here, I'd say to him, "Are you the same depressed, despairing man who couldn't sleep, who couldn't think about God because even thinking about Him made you moan in anguish? You thought God had changed, and here you are declaring Him the God of wonders! You're worshiping Him as the sacred God whose ways are holy. You've moved from dark to light."

Expressing Lament

As Asaph and other psalmists were teaching me to worship in the minor key of lament, I began to share what I was learning with the Ukrainian women in my Zoom group. These women listened intently as we discussed how Asaph dealt with his pain. After the teaching on lament, Olga, the leader of the group said, "Linda, this is very interesting. We have not heard these things before. I want to think more on them. I think this is what the people of Ukraine need." These women lived each day in a war for their very lives as Russian missiles bombed their homes and killed their husbands, brothers, fathers, and friends.

The idea of lament was unfamiliar to the Ukrainian women. Lament can take many different forms because our individual pain and relationships with God look different. I have found that the best way to learn our own voice of lament is to see how others have bravely cried out to God, chosen to remember, and stepped into worship.

A Mom's Lament

My friend and a communication coach Heidi Petak was grieving a difficult family relationship. The journey of lament helped her bring her honest pain to God and move toward trust and praise.

LAMENT

Oh, God, can't You hear me calling for help? For rescue? Do You have cotton in Your ears? Are Your hands tied up so You can't act and can't save? Do You not see my heartache, my tears, my sighing, my burden that is crushing my joy and my hope? Have You just decided we aren't worth it and You have more important things to do? Has Your arm been shortened, Your feet been placed into cement boots so You cannot act? Do You not care that we are desperate, waiting for Your miracle?

I will remember the works of the Lord, how You chose this child for us. I will remember the wonders of God, how You called my child out of darkness into Your marvelous light. I will remember the mercy of the Father, how You welcome the prodigal home. You do not shame us but celebrate our return. I will remember Your miraculous power; how You parted the sea to save Your people from their enemy; how You have conquered evil, death, and the grave by Your resurrection! I will remember that the endings of the stories You write are good.

Oh, God, I see Your radiance, Your white robes, Your glowing countenance. You are so bright! I fall to my knees at Your feet and press my face into the ground, wrapping my arms around Your ankles. You gently pick me up to look into Your loving eyes, and I understand. In an instant, I understand. Your eyes twinkle. Your mouth smiles—at me. Without a word, all my questions are answered before I even ask them. I stand in awe of You. Your love wraps me up with one glance, one smile, one embrace. I put my head on Your chest. I love Your heartbeat. My heart finally syncs up and beats with Yours. I am home.

My friend Shannon Adducci, a gifted singer-songwriter, also wrote a lament for her child in the form of a song. Listen to "He Loves You More"—it will bless your heart.[10]

A Believer's Lament

In his book *A Sacred Sorrow*, Michael Card weaves a beautiful, poetic lament that shows the same interplay between complaint, remembrance, and worship. In this lament, which of those elements do you notice as you go along?

A Lament: "You didn't fix me, You joined me!"

I acknowledge before You, Lord, the glaring gap in the difference between what I feel and what I believe.
Right now, I feel like You don't really care.
So many situations in my life are out of control.
Why don't You just fix them?
So much in and around me hurts right now.
Why don't You just heal them?
Were I willing to take more time to pray . . . from my side of things,
  this could become a shouting business.
DO SOMETHING!
But, You have already done something, haven't You?
You did what it took to become familiar with all the sorrows
  that I feel pressing in on me even this very moment.
You felt the gap between what You felt and what You believed, didn't You?
Jesus, I'm so sorry I said You didn't care.

*Is there anything I could say that would have caused You more
    pain than that?*
You didn't come to fix things for me, did You?
You came to join me.
Thank You.
Can I ask You one more thing?
*Would You, in the sacrament of this moment,
    enter right now into the holy of holies that is my hurt?*
Come in, not to fix but to simply be present.
*Be Immanuel inside that sacred, hurting place,
    even if it's for only a few precious moments.*
I can feel You now inside me Lord, Jesus.
I'm so sorry.
Thank You.[11]

These two laments reveal the sigh of healing that envelops us when we open our lives completely to the Holy Spirit and ask Him to place a finger on the scars that need to be offered up through lament.

The Surprise of Lament

What surprised me most about biblical lament is that it is never a place of being stuck—it's always forward moving, always advancing me into deeper trust in God. Like Asaph, my complaints moved me to remember. And as I reflected on who God is and what He has done, my remembrances moved me to worship.

Think of lament as a river of sorrow formed by your own tears. As you float on the river, the current beneath you moves toward the destination of greater faith in God. Sometimes you don't feel the movement, but it's there—because God is there. With each prayer of pain, each whisper of worship to God, you are carried along until one day you discover *I'm not in the same place I was. I'm in a new place, and I'm not sure how I got here.*

I've seen this happen in my sweet granddaughter Annika's life. About a year after she wrote the wrenching lament the day her mother died, her words began to move forward from grief to gratitude.

I'M GETTING TO KNOW YOU
I am getting to know you
All over again
Through the eyes and voices and hearts
Of other people
Through your handwriting in journals half finished
In closets full of your scent
And stories told through old friends
And long-lost letters read
I am getting to know my mother
In a way I never did before
I thought I was close to her then
But, oh, the things I get now to explore
I am so lucky to still be able
To get to know her even after she is gone
ANNIKA DUPUIS[12]

Discovering gratitude even in lament doesn't mean there won't be tough days. Or that the familiar sadness will never reappear. But I can promise you this: At some point, your many acts of faith will give way to a new dawn of hope.

Heart Skill
A LAMENT

Lament is a Heart Skill you'll use throughout your life. The important thing is to understand that lament is a process that God approves of and is a way in which He heals you. Write your own lament to God:

- ~ Cry out your complaint.
- ~ Choose to remember.
- ~ Worship God in His majesty.

CHAPTER 5

TRUST

*I know now, Lord, why you utter
no answer. You are yourself the answer.
Before your face questions die away.*

C. S. LEWIS

Trust

*A*REN'T YOU GLAD that lament is always forward moving? When we take our pain to God, He always leads us toward hope and deeper trust. If we don't turn to Him . . . well, we might find ourselves putting our trust in strange objects that can't actually help us at all.

My conversation with Jenny, a college girl, went like this:

"It doesn't matter what I believe in," said Jenny. "It's the believing that helps me."

"Explain to me just what you mean," I replied. "What do you believe in?"

"Oh, anything I want. Right now, I have faith in a big rock in my backyard."

"You're serious, a big rock really helps you?"

"Oh yes. If I just believe strongly enough, if I have enough faith that the rock will help me, it will. I stand in front of the big rock, close my eyes, and just believe that it will give me strength."

I explained to Jenny that the key to faith is the object of it. Christ is the only trustworthy object of faith. But Jenny wanted to believe in her rock. Rocks are convenient to believe in. They expect nothing, they command nothing, they require no obedience on the part of the "believer."

When you are in pain, you have to make sure that what you put your trust in is trustworthy. When I think about true faith—heartfelt, throw-yourself-in-with-complete-abandon faith—two important things come to mind:

1. Faith is rooted in God's character. He is holy. Wise. Just. Good. Merciful. Faithful. Sovereign. He is love. He loves me. He loves you.

2. Faith is based on God's character and God's Word, not on our feelings.

Or, as Hebrews 11:1 so beautifully puts it, "Faith is the assurance of things hoped for, the conviction of things not seen" (ESV). Jenny wanted to see the object of her faith, and she would trust in whatever felt good to her. But seeing something doesn't make it trustworthy. *Knowing* someone trustworthy—His character, what He has done, what He has revealed about Himself in His Word—makes all the difference.

My Trust Questions

I use the words *trust* and *faith* interchangeably in this chapter. The Greek word *pistis*, used throughout the New Testament, can refer to faith, trust, or confidence. These English words are all related in terms of how we express our belief in God.[1] We trust God because we have faith. We have faith because we trust Him.

Think with me about what it means for you, in your pain right now, to make a choice to trust God—not just a little bit or if you feel like it but with all your heart. We need to take this seriously because having faith is high on God's priority list.

Why is trust so important?

Trusting God blesses me (Psalm 84:12). Trusting brings me peace (Isaiah 26:3). It keeps me from being fearful (Psalm 56:3-4). It gives me power over the enemy (Luke 10:19-20). It infuses my life with the life of God (Jeremiah 17:5-8). And, as Hebrews 11:6 tells us, "Without faith it is impossible to please God." I love that my faith blesses me, but to think that it can also bless my God? To know that I can please Him and delight Him simply by trusting Him? Oh, I want that—don't you? I want to glorify my Abba and please Him with my life choices, even when making the choice to trust is hard.

Why is trust so hard?

Jerry Bridges, in his book *Trusting God*, says that trust is so hard because "we do not know the extent, the duration, or the frequency of the painful, adverse circumstances in which we must frequently trust God. We are always coping with the unknown."[2] If we could see into the future, it would be easier to trust God. Yet from our vantage point here on earth, we just can't see around the corner of our pain. But God can—because God lives in an everlasting now.

Oh, my friend, this truth about my God has so comforted my heart during my pain—my Abba Father has already lived all my tomorrows, and He has lived yours, too. I love how F. B. Meyer makes the eternity of God plain:

> This is the Blessed Life—not anxious to see far in front . . . not eager to choose the path . . . but quietly following behind the Shepherd, *one step at a time*. . . .
> [He] was always *ahead* of his sheep. He was down *in front*. Any attack upon them had to take him into account. Now God is down in front. He is in the tomorrows. It is tomorrow that fills men with dread. *God is there already*. All the tomorrows of our life have to pass Him before they can get to us.[3]

Did you fully take in all Meyer said? God is already in my tomorrows, in your tomorrows, in my daughter Robin's tomorrows as she faces new hard things about cancer. He is in your loved ones' tomorrows. That's why we can entrust them to Him and give Him the heavy load of all that might happen.

I have bought two plaques for my study to remind me of this truth. One says, "He is still God." The other says, "I trust the next chapter because I know the author." Holding the eternity of God deep in my heart has encouraged me as I've walked through my brain injury, Joy's death, and Robin's ongoing cancer journey. I want to trust God.

My Teacher of Trust

I've learned a lot about trust from a teacher who may seem strange to you. His name is Habakkuk, and he was an Old Testament prophet.

Why do I love Habakkuk? The reason is simple. God has met me in very personal ways in the pages of this hard-to-spell book of the Bible. The dates written in those pages span decades of my life. May 10, 1984, when my teens were in turmoil—which meant I was also in turmoil. November 28, 1999, when my granddaughter Sofia was born in Finland and struggling to live. January 2007, when I experienced my traumatic brain injury. The years 2020 and 2021, when both my daughters had cancer. All these dates recall painful situations where I had to cling to God, just like Habakkuk, whose name actually means "cling" or "embrace."[4]

Let me tell you a little about this incredible man. Habakkuk is the only prophet in the Bible who speaks only to God and no one else. All the other prophets speak to God and other people, but reading Habakkuk feels more like reading someone's diary than reading prophetic oratory. It's raw, real, personal. It's a book of deep struggle—an honest man trying to come to grips with what God is doing when God doesn't make sense at all. Yet it is also a book of hope.

Habakkuk is a short book—only three chapters. Here's how

the book unfolds: Chapter 1 explains Habakkuk's problems. In the opening pages, this dear prophet cries out to God and asks Him why He allows wicked practices to continue in Judah. God answers, but His answer is more confusing than the original question—and creates a bigger problem. Let me outline it for you:

> Problem #1: *God, why do You allow wicked practices to continue in Judah?* (Habakkuk 1:1-4)
> Answer #1: *I'm sending the Babylonians to take over Judah.* (Habakkuk 1:5-11)
> Problem #2: *God, how can You use people who are more evil than we are to punish us? Why, God? Why?* (Habakkuk 1:12-17)

Imagine that things in your country have gotten so bad—the people as a whole have wandered so far from God, indulged so gleefully in sins of violence and destructive behavior and cold viciousness—that you get on your knees and cry out to God to make it all stop. And God's response is to anoint the most vile person in the world—Vladimir Putin, perhaps, or Kim Jong Un, or the figurehead leader of a godless terror network—as judge to wage war and destroy your country. How would you respond? You might simply scream, "No! God, You can't mean that! Don't punish our evil with people who are far more evil than we are. That just doesn't make sense!"

Habakkuk does just that. He screams "Why?" at God and says, "I don't understand You." He asks *"Why,* God?" three times (see Habakkuk 1:13-14, NASB). But then he says,

> I will take my stand at my watchpost
>   and station myself on the tower,

and look out to see what he will say to me,
and what I will answer concerning my complaint.
HABAKKUK 2:1, ESV

Often the first thing we want to do when we don't understand God is to push ahead with our own agenda. But Habakkuk yields to God even though he's confused and frustrated. As he does, he shows us the way of trust: retreat, remember, recommit.

Retreat

First, Habakkuk retreats to a quiet, sacred place. Determined to be alone with God, he crawls up into a watchtower and waits upon the Lord. Do you have a place where you can retreat and be still before the Lord? Maybe it's a special place outdoors where you walk and wrestle through questions with God, a specific chair in your house, or a closet you've turned into a prayer haven. For me, it's the ottoman in my office. I kneel over it as I listen to the Lord. I was there in the middle of the night last night. As I bow my body and soul, my spirit sighs, and I am in the presence of the Holy One.

Remember

The words "look out to see" (Habakkuk 2:1) mean "watch intently"—as though you're leaning forward in eager anticipation, sitting on the edge of your seat, knowing something is going to happen. It's like Habakkuk preaches to himself, *Habakkuk, remember—this is your God from everlasting. He is your holy God. You've trusted Him before; you can trust Him now. All is confusing right now, but God is still God. Be still, and wait expectantly for Him alone!* Preaching God's truth to ourselves is a good thing to do.

Recommit

When we are in pain, we must always come back to the truth of who God is. Understanding Hebrew grammar helps us see how Habakkuk did this. In Hebrew, the imperfect tense often communicates incompleteness, or action still ongoing. Here Habakkuk is likely saying, "I will take my stand, and I will continue to take my stand." With each "I will" in this verse, Habakkuk is probably stressing continuation: *You're the Holy God—I will wait—and continue to wait—for Your answer.*

Why am I making such a big deal about Hebrew grammar? Because knowing this has helped me. In Habakkuk 2:1, Habakkuk waits. In verse 2, God's answer comes. I don't think the answer came quickly. We don't know how long Habakkuk waited and sat at his guard post. Personally, I believe he waited a long time. Maybe it's because I know what it is to wait on God to answer, and I bet you do too.

Habakkuk wanted a specific, personal answer, just like we do when we're waiting on and trusting God. And God gives Habakkuk an amazing answer—it isn't specific or personal, but it is clear. *My word for you, Habakkuk, is this: "The just shall live by his faith"* (Habakkuk 2:4, KJV). This phrase is so important that the New Testament writers quote it three times (Romans 1:17; Galatians 3:11; Hebrews 10:38).

Moreover, God also essentially says in verse 4, *Habakkuk, I see these proud Babylonians. Their hearts are not right. I know that. Leave them to Me; but as for you, Habakkuk, trust Me.* What's Habakkuk's response? He chooses to recommit—to trust God even when God doesn't make sense to him.

Expressions of Trust

Habakkuk still doesn't have satisfactory answers to his questions, but he chooses to trust God as he pens one of the most profound prayers of praise in the Bible:

> Though the fig tree should not blossom
> And there be no fruit on the vines,
> Though the yield of the olive should fail
> And the fields produce no food,
> Though the flock should be cut off from the fold
> And there be no cattle in the stalls,
> Yet I will exult in the LORD,
> I will rejoice in the God of my salvation.
> The Lord GOD is my strength,
> And He has made my feet like hinds' feet,
> And makes me walk on my high places.
> HABAKKUK 3:17-19, NASB

Habakkuk lists everything that gives him security and sustenance. His list is probably very different from yours or mine because he lived in an agrarian culture. What would that list look like for you or me? Could we join him in saying, "Even if everything is taken . . . yet . . ."?

Yet . . . "I'm singing joyful praise to GOD."

Yet . . . "I'm turning cartwheels of joy to my Savior God" (Habakkuk 3:19, MSG).

Such jubilant praise! The Babylonians are still advancing. Habakkuk is terrified of what's about to transpire. And yet he is spinning around for joy in his God.

I call Habakkuk 3:17-19 my Trust Verses. Trust Verses are

Scriptures that are written on your heart because you have memorized them; they are verses you turn to throughout your life to keep you looking into the eyes of the Holy One. These three verses have been an anchor in my life that has kept me grounded in who God is no matter what I'm facing. On March 19, 2021—the day Joy entered heaven—with tears, I opened my Bible to Habakkuk 3:17-19 and entered that date below the others in the margin.

My *though*s to God were different from Habakkuk's, but my cry of trust was the same:

> *Though I may never understand why both my precious daughters had cancer,*
> *though I may never understand why Joy died,*
> *though my heart continues to feel this scorching pain,*
> *yet I will exult in the Lord,*
> *I will rejoice in the God of my salvation.*
> *The Lord God is my strength!*

Did I ask God to heal Joy? Of course! His answer was no. I like it better when God says yes than when He says no. But I learned a few things from Habakkuk. I learned that trust is a choice. I can choose to trust or not to trust. I also learned that it's possible to go beyond trust to worship. Habakkuk defied his feelings of fear and confusion and chose instead to spin around with joy and delight in his God. His faith became worship before his mighty God. I want this too! I want to delight in my God and honor God by worshiping Him even when I'm confused and afraid, even when I don't have answers to my *why*s.

Do you have Trust Verses that anchor you? Do you have a verse or a passage of Scripture that causes hope to rise in you and helps you trust God even when you feel like throwing in the towel? Let me introduce you to a few friends whose expressions of trust—a Trust Song and Trust Verses—have helped them turn toward God when life has been hard.

Laura: A Trust Song

Laura Story wrote a beautiful Trust Song that deeply ministered to me during some of the darkest days of my grieving. I had the joy of speaking at a women's retreat in Georgia where Laura was the worship leader for the weekend. We had several chances to talk. What had unfolded in her life made my heart ache.

Her husband, Martin, had surgery for a brain tumor when he was twenty-eight years old. After the surgery, Martin could not work; he could not drive. He basically had no short-term memory.

"We had such hopes and dreams!" Laura told me. "Martin was pursuing his master's degree. We wanted children. Now is that even possible?"

I hugged Laura and prayed for her. As I did, my heart filled with compassion. What does a marriage look like when the husband has trouble functioning? What does it look like for her to be the financial provider for their family? What does trusting God look like when you're never going to have the life you both dreamed of?[5]

I'll tell you in a single word what it looked like for Laura: blessings. "Blessings" is a song that God gave to Laura in direct response to the trials in her and her husband's lives. Through the lyrics she asks questions, just as Habakkuk did—and she wonders: What if the hard things in her life were actually blessings in disguise?[6]

Laura also wrote a thought-provoking book, *When God Doesn't*

Fix It. In her chapter called "Why?" she says this was the single word that haunted her most.[7] She felt that if she just had an answer to that question, she would feel better. But at some point, Laura realized she was asking the wrong question. Instead of asking why, she needed to ask *how*.

~ How might God use your current trial to glorify Him?
~ How might God use your weakness, infirmity, or disability to display His power?
~ How might God use your hard circumstances to show you something about Him—or you?
~ How might God make your mess into a message?[8]

If you are stuck in *why*, maybe now would be a good time for you to find a quiet place, nestle down with God, and talk to Him about these *how* questions. Connecting with God and seeing with His eyes is how we learn to trust Him.

Gary: Habakkuk 3:17-19

Gary DeSalvo's Trust Verses are the same as Habakkuk's and mine. Gary pastored a church in Temple, Texas. Under his leadership and his wife's, the congregation grew from forty to four thousand.

Then one visit to the eye doctor turned Gary's life upside down. The diagnosis was ocular melanoma. The doctor removed his eye, but there's no cure for this kind of cancer.

What do you do when you are officially handed a death notice? Bev, his amazingly positive wife, determined that the whole family would live each of his remaining days with joy and continue to love one another well.

Even though the doctors gave no hope, Gary's Trust Verses helped him have hope in the God in whom he trusted. One Sunday he stood before the congregation and read these words from a large TV screen:

Lord, if it will be to Your glory, heal suddenly.
If it will glorify You more—heal gradually.
If it will glorify You even more—
may Your servant remain sick awhile,
and if it will glorify Your Name still more—
take him to Yourself in heaven.

Gary died several months later. Would Gary have liked to be directly, immediately, gloriously healed by God? Of course. Would Bev have liked Gary to live so they could be joyously ministering together in their church? Of course. Would I like my Joy to be here for Christmas when the whole family gathers? Do I yearn for her to be present for Annika's wedding? Oh, my heart hurts even as I write that. Of course I want that. But remember what I said earlier about having eternity in our hearts? Even though it's hard, we've got to lift our eyes to heaven and remember that there is a bigger story at play.

Oh, my friend, God's Word is powerful. Healing. Hopeful. His Word is living and active—it infuses life into you and refreshes your spirit (see, for example, Psalm 138:7; Hebrews 12:3). God's Word is a hiding place (Psalm 119:114). It revives you when you're in despair (Psalm 119:107). When you feel like giving up, God's Word is a lamp to your feet and a light to your path by bringing hope and guidance (Psalm 119:105).

Alaine: Romans 12:2

My close friend Alaine has taught me much about trusting God. Many sexually abused women look to Alaine as a beacon of hope. They hear what happened to her yet see her joy and think maybe they also can experience joy again.

Alaine's childhood was tragic. From the ages of five to thirteen, she was a victim of family trafficking. It always happened in their home, away from prying eyes, from those who might help, from those who might care. How do you heal from this lack of protection and love from the ones who should be your shelter? How do you grow up to be sane? Where can you find transformation?

Alaine discovered it in God's Word in Romans 12:2 (NASB):

> Do not be conformed to this world, but be transformed
> by the renewing of your mind, so that you may prove
> what the will of God is, that which is good and acceptable
> and perfect.

Do you see it? Transformation is possible when a mind is renewed. Alaine needed a new mind—but also a new heart. Alaine knew that planting Scripture in her mind would replace the traumatic images of the past.

So what, you may wonder, did she memorize? A few psalms? The book of Philippians?

I can hardly type these words because what my friend Alaine did so amazes me. She planted *the whole New Testament* plus *all the Psalms* in her mind and heart. Amazing! More than a hundred and fifty psalms and twenty-seven books in the New Testament continue to lead her into trust—kicking out the evil and birthing hope in its place. I haven't memorized all hundred and fifty of the Psalms or twenty-seven books of the Bible—have you? Probably not! God asked Alaine to do this because we are transformed by the renewing of our minds and Alaine's mind so needed rebuilding.

I asked Alaine, "How did you do this remarkable thing?" She told me, "Twenty minutes a day for twenty years. Then I reviewed what I had memorized for twenty more years." That's how dear Alaine renewed her mind and heart and became a woman of joy and peace who leads other broken women to peace.[9]

Small Steps toward Trust

I'm wondering what you're thinking right now. Perhaps for some of you, what you've been reading is hard. You can't relate to a woman who memorizes entire books of the Bible—in fact, you aren't sure you want to memorize one verse, because you're not sure God is 100 percent trustworthy. You can't imagine praising God with the loss you carry. You feel He's let you down. You have many doubts about many things!

Still, there's a tiny part of you that wants to believe. But where to begin? My friend, you can begin here, begin now. Hand your tiny sliver of belief to God, and ask Him to make up the difference. Like the man who cried out to Jesus, say, "I believe; help my unbelief!" (Mark 9:24, ESV).

Trust is a series of small steps. A practice like having a Trust Verse can be a starting place, or a middle place, or an ending place. No matter where you are with trusting God in your pain, you can move one foot forward, a simple act of faith toward the One who is faithful. Every step of trust becomes a firm reminder to put your hope in God.

I want to leave you with some words from my friend Alaine:

I asked all my life, *God, where were You . . . when all the horrible things were done to me?* But this morning, as I drive to the university where I am a professor, God answers my question. I sense God speaking, so I pull my car over to the side of the road and listen. His message is clear. Not a voice but a knowing in my spirit. He tells me four things:

Every time you prayed, I heard. How kind of Him to tell me that.

Every time you wept, I wept. So I was never alone with my tears!

Your finite mind cannot understand why I gave humans the power to choose either good or evil.

The fourth thing God says leads me to a choice.

Do you trust Me?

Beside the road, with my car engine still running, I hear from the God who had kept me alive for all those years. With tears running down my face, I say,

Thank You, God, for hanging on to me.
Thank You, God, for keeping me sane.
Thank You, God, for healing me.
Thank You, God, for using my pain to bring hope and healing to others.[10]

Trust is a gift we lay at the feet of the Lord we love. I hear in my head Christina Rossetti's lovely lyric "What can I give Him, poor as I am?"[11] Faith is the perfect gift I can give as a sojourner on this earth. In heaven faith will not be needed. Every pain will be explained, every mystery solved. My faith will become sight.

But today I'm stuck here on earth, and I see only dimly as through a dirty glass . . . yet I see Him—and He is *God, Lord, Yahweh, the great I AM, Jesus, my Holy Spirit*. For a short time, I feel like I see clearly. I see Him in my spirit when I say . . .

I trust You.
Even if I don't understand.
Even if I can't see what You're doing.
Even if my heart still hurts.

. . . and my Abba sings loudly over me with delight.

Heart Skill
A VERSE

Ask God to show you your personal Trust Verse(s) that can encourage you today and guide you as you seek to trust Him in the coming years. Memorize this verse. Say it often. As you do, allow the power of God's Word to refresh and strengthen your faith.

CHAPTER 6

FORGIVENESS

The person who gains the most from forgiveness is the person who does the forgiving.

R. T. KENDALL

Forgiveness

FORGIVENESS

*W*HEN YOU TRUST GOD, you have the courage and strength to forgive others, even when they wound you in unspeakable ways. That's what I needed—because I had a problem.

As a young woman, I hated my father.

You read that right: I hated him.

But it was the truth.

Every little girl longs for a daddy to protect her, to support her dreams. A father who thinks she hung the moon. My father was the exact opposite. He thought his brand of bourbon hung the moon. He frightened my younger brother and me with his fits of rage and shouted horrible lies about my sweet mother. His violence made our home a living hell. Sometimes the police came. On those nights, my mom, my brother, and I fled to a motel, where we could sleep in safety.

His actions made me hate him. When I was in high school, he pulled me out of dances drunk. He cut up my clothes. He smashed my perfume bottles on the cement. He drank away my money for college. He tore up my college applications. He staggered across my high school graduation stage in Bermuda shorts, drunk out of his mind.

But if his actions shamed and humiliated me, his words hurt even more. He called me "an everyday, ordinary, garden variety whore."[1] And it was a lie. I was an honor student, head cheerleader, and trying to be a good girl.

Our home was falling apart, but no one knew. I was a good actress. I looked good on the outside, but inside I was filled with hate. I had no answers about how to handle the scathing resentment I felt toward my father for what he'd done to our family.

While I tried to figure out how to deal with my father hate, a huge ball of pain inside me grew as I watched my boyfriend of two years die of cancer. It was all too much. I had no skills to cope with the cauldron of roiling emotions inside me. So I shoved the pain down, put a smile on my face, and left for a college far, far away.

At college, my life took a drastic turn. Jesus found me! I learned that He loved, cherished, and valued me. He held out the gift of eternal life to me. He forgave my sins.

Jesus' unconditional love and forgiveness overwhelmed me. I danced through many months delighting in this forgiveness until one day I sensed that it was time for me to forgive someone. Guess who my God pointed to? The one I hated: my father.

By this time, my father and mother had divorced. I pictured him in his apartment, watching TV, smoking three packs of Camels a day, and drinking bourbon and milk for breakfast. This narcissistic man hadn't asked for forgiveness.

Really, God? Forgive him?

Yes, Linda, you heard right. Good hearing.

But God, why? He doesn't deserve it.

Daughter, did you deserve My gifts to you of forgiveness and eternal life?

Okay, God, I get it.

It was time to let go of my hate. I bowed my head and prayed. I don't remember the exact words I spoke, but it was something like "God, I want to be free! Take the hate, the pain—I want to forgive like Jesus did."

As I prayed that prayer of forgiveness, the pain and anger inside me released its death grip on me. Did that mean I was instantly healed—that I never felt pain again because of my father's actions and words? No. Truthfully, I've had some hard days as I've written here about the harm I experienced because of my father's alcoholism. I rarely talk about the early decades of my life, and doing it now has resurfaced painful memories and caused me to see new losses. So I had to do what I'm writing about: I had to acknowledge the losses, grieve them, trust God even when things didn't make sense, and forgive—again.

Now I'm thinking about you, my friend. Can you relate? Is there someone in your life who has hurt you so deeply that the pain reverberates through the years and you feel like you will never get over it because new losses continue to surface? Do the layers of loss seem endless? Do you feel like you are stuck in a cycle of loss, lament, trust, and forgiveness?

If so, you're not alone. But rather than reject this cycle, I've come to embrace it and to see it as a way for God to teach me to live a lifestyle of love and forgiveness. This is what Jesus modeled so beautifully. It's what God wants for you—and for me—because a heart of forgiveness makes us more like Jesus.

A Lifestyle of Forgiveness

What does it really mean to forgive? According to psychologists, forgiveness is "a conscious, deliberate decision to release feelings of resentment or vengeance toward a person or group who has harmed you, regardless of whether they actually deserve your forgiveness."[2]

Forgiveness is not easy. God asked me to forgive one evil man, and that was beyond hard. But think about Jesus! He hung on a cross and forgave all humanity for every shameful act they'd ever committed—past, present, and future. Do you think that was hard?

Humanity was cruel to Jesus, especially in those last hours of His life. They stripped Him bare. Maybe you think, like in the crucifixion images you've seen in stained glass windows at church or in museum art, that a loincloth covered Him. Wrong.

He was naked.

Exposed.

Vulnerable.

God on a cross.

In addition to stripping Him, humanity whipped, beat, mocked, and spit upon Jesus. Then they nailed God to a cross. They laughed and jeered. And where were Jesus' heart and eyes? He looked at the thief on the cross to His left and the one to His right and offered them forgiveness. He looked at the evil, insulting, vile men below, gambling for His clothing, and at the judgmental religious leaders approving of His despair and said some of the holiest words ever spoken: "Father, forgive them, for they do not know what they are doing" (Luke 23:34). Jesus lived forgiveness during His life and breathed it in the moments before His death.

When nails pierce your hands and feet, when death stands ready to whisk you away, you measure your words carefully. What was our Savior's final word to us? *Forgive.*

Forgiveness cost Jesus His life. It will cost us as well.

When the disciple Peter wanted to know the limits of forgiveness, he asked Jesus, "How many times shall I forgive my brother or sister who sins against me? Up to seven times?" (Matthew 18:21). The rabbis said to forgive three times, so Peter thought he was being exceptionally virtuous by suggesting seven.

Jesus' answer must have astounded Peter: "I say to you, not up to seven times, but seventy times seven" (Matthew 18:22, AMP) Jesus was not suggesting 490 as the magic number. He was saying, "Keep on forgiving. Forgive as many times as it takes."

Then Jesus, the master storyteller, followed His answer with a parable:

> "The Kingdom of Heaven can be compared to a king who decided to bring his accounts up to date with servants who had borrowed money from him. In the

process, one of his debtors was brought in who owed him millions of dollars. He couldn't pay, so his master ordered that he be sold—along with his wife, his children, and everything he owned—to pay the debt.

"But the man fell down before his master and begged him, 'Please, be patient with me, and I will pay it all.' Then his master was filled with pity for him, and he released him and forgave his debt.

"But when the man left the king, he went to a fellow servant who owed him a few thousand dollars. He grabbed him by the throat and demanded instant payment.

"His fellow servant fell down before him and begged for a little more time. 'Be patient with me, and I will pay it,' he pleaded. But his creditor wouldn't wait. He had the man arrested and put in prison until the debt could be paid in full.

"When some of the other servants saw this, they were very upset. They went to the king and told him everything that had happened. Then the king called in the man he had forgiven and said, 'You evil servant! I forgave you that tremendous debt because you pleaded with me. Shouldn't you have mercy on your fellow servant, just as I had mercy on you?' Then the angry king sent the man to prison to be tortured until he had paid his entire debt.

"That's what my heavenly Father will do to you if you refuse to forgive your brothers and sisters from your heart."
MATTHEW 18:23-35, NLT

Jesus is serious about forgiveness. When we don't forgive, we are throwing ourselves into prison and choosing intense inner torment. As Chuck Swindoll says, "A Christian is a candidate for confinement—and unspeakable suffering—until he or she fully and completely forgives others . . . even when others are in the wrong."³ Forgiveness is the key that unlocks the door of resentment and the handcuffs of hate. Forgiveness breaks the chains of bitterness and the shackles of selfishness.

The Hardest Kind of Forgiveness

During your lifetime, you will have to forgive many people. Maybe you'll forgive a lovely church member who isn't acting like Jesus. Or a neighbor who lets his dog continually poop in your yard. It could even be a stranger who sues you for emotional trauma after a fender bender. Forgiveness is always a challenge because it requires humility on our part, but the most difficult people to forgive are usually those closest to us, the ones we rub shoulders with day after day.

I shared earlier about how hard it was to forgive my father. But it's also hard to forgive others with the power to deeply wound—a husband, an adult child, a mother. I want to share with you how three friends walked through forgiveness in these important relationships. I pray their stories will connect with your own pain and inspire you to keep forgiving and keep trusting God so that your own heart doesn't become bitter.

Forgiving a Husband

I'll begin with Shannon, my friend and neighbor. As I was reeling from both Joy and Robin having cancer in the middle of a worldwide pandemic, Shannon was having her own crisis as she struggled to forgive her husband.

Shannon's father was an Army general, and she was an Army nurse, so it made sense that she'd fall in love with and marry Rob, a West Point graduate. Rob professed a passionate love for Jesus and for Shannon. They planned to model their life and family after Christ. But what they didn't plan on was a health crisis. Six months after their wedding, Shannon was diagnosed with multiple sclerosis (MS).

This spunky woman gave birth to two sons, but eventually her body betrayed her. When her oldest son was in second grade, the tremors in her hands and legs and the confusion in her brain ended her ability to drive a vehicle.

Shannon and Rob moved into our neighborhood when their sons were in their twenties. By this time, Shannon was noticeably disabled. She wore a brace on her left leg and walked with the aid of a walker.

From Shannon's perspective, her marriage was good. That's why she was so shocked when Rob told her he was fed up with her MS. He was frustrated that she couldn't bike or golf like his friends' wives. "You can't meet any of my needs," he told her. And before she could utter the word *betrayal*, her husband of nearly thirty years walked out the door and into the arms of another woman he had waiting in the wings.

I'll let Shannon tell you in her own words about her process of forgiveness.

> I was in complete shock. I couldn't believe that this man with whom I'd shared my life and raised a family would up and leave! He was an elder and small group leader in our church. How could he play the role of a servant of God and break his covenant promise with God? With me?
>
> I had many questions. How would I survive? I couldn't live alone because my disabilities required someone to assist me. But there was no one. My husband was gone.

The pandemic-imposed isolation prohibited people from connecting. I felt utterly helpless. So I crawled into God's lap, and He held me. Every day I read His Word. It gave me what I needed. One. Hour. At. A time. Then the next day I'd start all over again.

Some days I barely functioned. I felt so broken, like I wasn't enough. I was angry with Rob's lies and empty promises. One day I read Ephesians 4:32: "Be kind to one another, tenderhearted, forgiving one another, as God in Christ forgave you" (ESV). But how could I be tenderhearted toward Rob after all the pain he'd caused me?

Then I read *Total Forgiveness* by R. T. Kendall. The author made it crystal clear that even though I wanted to hold a grudge and point a finger at Rob, God desired for me to lay my grievances aside and forgive. Easy? No. But I knew I had to do it.

I know unforgiveness can block my destiny and hinder my fellowship with God. I wanted no part of that. It took a while, but I came to the point where I put Rob into the hands of God. I released my pain, shame, and blame. It was agonizing and cost me many tears, but, after three years, I can look back and see that I'm a different person because I followed Jesus and His command to forgive.

I so admire Shannon. As I look out my office window, I see her walking with a walker, smiling with confidence and waving at everyone she sees. Shannon has gone through more pain and loss than many people face in a lifetime. Things didn't turn out as she'd hoped. And yet, today, she says this about her life: "I'm better, not bitter."

Forgiving an Adult Child

If you were to visit a certain church in Colorado, you'd likely meet Claire, a fiery blue-eyed redhead who works there. She'd welcome you warmly and, as you saw the light in her eyes and the joy that radiates from her smile, you might think, *She's so vibrant—life must be great for her.* You'd be wrong. A churning pain twists Claire's stomach, a pain she carries on behalf of her twenty-year-old son, Nathan.

I'll let Claire tell you in her own words about why the pain she carries demands that she live a lifestyle of forgiveness.

> All I ever really wanted was to be a good mom to my son. I couldn't have children, so my husband and I adopted Nathan when he was a year old. The moment I held him in my arms, I fell in love! I kissed each tiny finger and tugged each perfectly formed toe. In that moment, I knew I'd do anything for my son—even die for him.
>
> I love Jesus, so when Nathan was little, I began telling him stories about Him. At bedtime he'd say, "Oh Mama, tell me the one about the blind man." Or "Can we do the fishes-and-loaves story tonight?"
>
> My tenderhearted child became a middle schooler. I loved cheering him on in baseball and football. I was always the team mom—it seemed like we constantly had a houseful of young boys laughing and roughhousing.
>
> But in high school, something changed. Nathan stopped going to church with us. He rejected his dad and me as "too traditional." He began hanging out with a bad crowd. He started using drugs. He sold drugs. He lied to me about who he was with and where he was going. He

even stole the jewelry my mom had given me and sold it for drugs. One night, a SWAT team of police officers showed up at 3:00 a.m. with lights flashing and guns drawn, demanding to speak to my son. That was a tough one to explain to my neighbors!

I was so angry. I felt so much loss on so many levels. Everything I'd hoped for him was swirling down a drain. Now a prison sentence hung over his head.

We'd tried everything we knew, and nothing seemed to work. Nathan had pastoral and professional counseling. We spent a fortune on rehab programs. We joined a support group for parents of troubled teens, set boundaries, and disciplined him in every loving way we knew how. Oh, the ocean of tears I cried as I begged Jesus, "Please, please, please! Rescue my son!"

I prayed thousands of prayers for him, and God always seemed to bring me back to two things: *Love him. Forgive him.* First Corinthians 13:5 says that love "keeps no record of wrongs." Jesus didn't keep a record of my wrongs, so I had no right to keep a record of Nathan's wrongs. Each week I'd write on a sheet of paper the things he'd done or said that had hurt me, the losses his choices had cost me. I'd grieve each hurt. After I'd gone through the entire list, I'd rip up the paper and throw it in the trash. This kept my heart clean; I could handle the next crisis.

I don't know what the future holds, but I choose to keep hoping, keep forgiving, keep trusting that God will one day return our prodigal son to us.[4]

I've talked to moms and grandmoms around the world—their stories are different, but the gut-twisting hurt is all too often the same. It all spells P-A-I-N. When you've given your life to your child, it hurts to have your love rejected, whether rashly or softly. But like Jesus, we choose to keep no record of wrongs. Refusing to be offended rips up the root of bitterness. Like Claire, you can become a victor rather than a victim.

Forgiving a Mother

I met Ginger twelve years ago, and words are not sufficient to describe who she is. But I can tell you that she's brave. Courageous. And God-transformed.

Before I ask Ginger to tell you her story in her own words, I need to warn you that what she shares could be triggering for some. If accounts of abuse spark memories or trauma in you that you are not yet ready to face, please prayerfully consider whether you should stop reading here. It's okay to skip to the Heart Skill at the end of this chapter. Ask the Holy Spirit to show you what is best and what is safe for you.

While Ginger's story is tragic, it is also one of the most powerfully redeeming messages I've ever heard about how to forgive someone who has deeply hurt you.

> As a child, I did not know my birth father. When my mother married my stepfather when I was eight years old, I was excited to finally have a dad. This man considered himself a good person because he was a churchgoer. He had me memorizing the Lord's Prayer, Psalm 23, and a few other Scriptures and prayers. We even had a plaque that hung in our home that read, "What does the LORD require of you? To act justly and to love mercy and and to walk humbly with your God" (Micah 6:8).

But my stepfather was not who he pretended to be. Evil unfolded behind closed doors. It didn't take long for him to begin abusing me physically and sexually. My stepfather's drinking caused his abuse to escalate, and he became unbearably debased to the point of torture. For instance, he pulled me around the house by my ears and punched me in the side of the head. My ears became disfigured from chronic abuse. My mother stood by and watched in silence.

When I was sixteen, we moved from New Jersey to Ohio. I did not know anyone in this new state. I was not allowed to go to school and spent the next two years locked in my bedroom with no outside contact. I was not allowed to wear clothes inside the house. I was only given bread and water to eat.

I cannot recall a time my mother defended me. She stripped me of necessities and left me completely isolated and alone. Together, she and my stepfather shaved off my hair so that my disfigured ears stuck out even more.

One day in a drunken rage, my stepfather stabbed me in the back three times with a steak knife, missing my spine by a quarter of an inch. My mother dressed my wounds and sent me back into the prison of my room. When she put bandages over the stab wounds, I felt the tiniest glimmer of hope that maybe she cared for me. I lost that hope the day she, too, became sexually violent with me.

How could she do this to her own flesh and blood? Why did she harm me instead of protect me? Why did she do nothing when my stepfather abused me? I loathed her. I loathed my existence.

Hope came to me through a Bible on my bookshelf in my bedroom. When I picked it up, I wasn't even sure I believed in God. But as I began reading the Psalms, I felt like the author perfectly described my own emotions—hopelessness, despair, and the fear of death. The only difference between us was that he continually asked God to rescue him from his enemies. The psalmist had a hope that I knew nothing about!

I put God to the test one day and prayed, *God, if You are real, get me out of here.*

God began answering my prayer through my mother and stepfather's greed. They told me I could eat when I got a job. He answered with a job at a factory. The day I came home with my first paycheck, I packed a few things in a duffle bag and left. I have never been back or had a relationship with my mom or stepfather since.

But my newfound freedom soon became a prison. When a young woman has been the victim of sexual and physical abuse, she thinks she deserves nothing, so she doesn't know how to make good choices. I prostituted myself to pay for a place to sleep and for drugs to numb my pain.

After a year of living like this, I encountered a friend I used to party with. She had stopped using drugs and invited me to go to church with her. I didn't want to go, but I went anyway. A gentleman there asked if he could pray for me. He asked me to repeat the words of his prayer. Because I am a people pleaser, I did this just to please him, but as I echoed his words, the presence of the Lord fell upon me. God was inviting me into a personal relationship with Him. I said yes to God, and slowly my life took a different path.

CHOOSING TO FORGIVE

As I was coming to grips with the true depth of the abuse, I experienced rage and hate with a force I had not felt before. The intensity of these emotions energized me and made me feel strong. They gave me a sense of power.

After becoming a Christian, I learned I needed to forgive others if I wanted to be forgiven. I believed all I had to do was speak the three simple words *I forgive you*. It wasn't until years later that I realized these words were empty, spoken out of duty rather than a heart change. Now God was challenging me to lay my anger and rage at His feet and forgive my evil abusers. But how?

Adults who were supposed to love and nurture me had instead abused me. If for some wild reason my mother repented, I would find it very difficult to forgive her—but if she never acknowledged her sinful, evil actions? It's so much harder to forgive when a person has no intention of admitting their sin.

Yet that was exactly what God was asking me to do.

Initially, I pled my case before God and tried to figure out how I could be exempt from what seemed to be an unrealistic command. I prayed and searched the Scriptures about forgiveness. Nothing let me off the hook.

For honest and true forgiveness to take place, I could not repress, minimize, or make excuses for the things that my mother had done to me. I could not demand that justice be done here on earth. I could not demand that God make this easy for me.

I knew I had to take practical steps to move toward forgiving my mother. Forgiving her did not excuse her behavior or culpability for her actions, but it would free me of the bitterness that had been suffocating me and stifling my spiritual and emotional growth.

GINGER'S FORGIVENESS CEREMONY

I asked God to show me what I could do to put my thoughts and convictions into action. The Lord showed me that I needed to bury my mother's sins against me along with my sins against her. So in the spring of 2015, before a small group of close friends, I named every sin she had committed against me. I spoke forgiveness over each one. Then I placed a drop of lavender oil on a cloth to represent its cleansing from my heart. I wrote my own sins of unforgiveness, hatred, rage, resentment, and bitterness against my mother on a rock. As my friends looked on, I wrapped the cloth around the rock and buried these objects in my backyard garden. Then I planted a lavender bush on top of the grave. My friends and I sang "Amazing Grace" together. And I read aloud this proclamation, to which my friends all signed their names as witnesses of my decision.

This day, May 6, 2015, I have publicly forgiven my mother of the sins she perpetrated against me. I have buried her sins along with my sins of resentment, bitterness, and the desire for revenge.

I ask You, Father God, to forgive my sin of wanting to see her pay for her sins and for desiring her spiritual death.

I ask that You make Yourself known to her so that she can experience the same newness of life that You have sacrificed to give to me.

Thank You for the undeserving forgiveness You have given in my life and for the gift of living with You forever.

When I struggle with future moments of unforgiveness, may this statement of truth be a constant reminder of what I have surrendered to You.

I love You, Father, Jesus, and Holy Spirit.

Each time I look at that lavender bush, I'm reminded that my mother's sins are no longer mine to carry. They are in God's hands; her actions are now His concern. Even today, when the enemy tries to remind me of a sin of hers I had not included on my list, I tell him, "No! It's finished," and I point to the lavender plant.

Unforgiveness is a curse, but the joy and liberty that I've experienced since I forgave my mother is a tangible blessing. I thank God for these four things:

- ~ Because of the abuse, I know God on a deeper level.
- ~ Through pain, God revealed His unexplainable love to me.
- ~ I have experienced the sweet fellowship of suffering with Christ (Philippians 3:10).
- ~ God caused me to be grateful and to worship Him because He loves me so deeply. As He continues to work in my heart, my mind, and my stubborn will, I continue to make choices to be free. Oh, there is such freedom!

Ginger's story makes me want to weep, not only for the abuse she suffered, but also over the beautiful way she forgave.

Whom do you need to forgive? A father? A husband? A mother, a sibling, or your grown child? A relative? A friend or colleague? Don't wait. Ginger, Claire, Shannon, and I all agree: Forgive now, because every moment you delay forgiveness, you allow bitterness to accumulate inside you. No matter what pain you've experienced, please don't let bitterness poison you.

Will you pray with me now?

Lord Jesus, help me, help me. This is so hard. You see how hurt I am. I want to let this go, to forgive, to be like You. By the power of Your Holy Spirit, I now release my hate. I want to be free! Thank You for hearing my prayer.

Heart Skill
A LIFESTYLE

Love . . . keeps no record of wrongs.
1 CORINTHIANS 13:4-5

Begin your lifestyle of forgiveness today by doing these three things:

1. *Commit.* From this day forward, by the power of the Holy Spirit, meet every offense with an attitude of Jesus-like forgiveness.

2. *Write and rip.* On a piece of paper, write every grievance in your mind or heart that you are holding against someone. Grieve the pain, then rip up your list and throw it in the trash.

3. *Repeat.* Put a reminder in your phone for a heart check on the first of every month. If offenses clutter your heart, repeat the steps above.

CHAPTER 7

ENCOURAGEMENT

But David encouraged himself in the LORD his God.
1 SAMUEL 30:6, KJV

Encouragement

ENCOURAGEMENT

A STORY IS TOLD about the devil having a garage sale. On one table he laid out some of his tools with prices attached to them.

Anger: $100

Resentment: $400

Hatred: $600

Lust: $1,000

One very used tool at the end of the table had no price tag. Late in the day, a middle-aged woman asked the devil about the old, worn-out tool. "What do you call that ugly, old thing?"

"Discouragement," smirked the devil. "It's not for sale."

"Who would want it?" asked the woman. "It looks worthless."

"Oh no," the devil sneered. "This is my favorite tool because so few realize it belongs to me. Nothing paralyzes a person like discouragement. When I use this tool, a woman can't pray. She can't worship. I've won because she only has enough energy to feel sorry for herself."

"No," the devil said. "I'll never sell my favorite tool, because it's just too effective."[1]

I can't begin to count the number of times the devil has used this tool on me—and I suspect he's also used it on you.

I remember when I first understood the true meaning of the word *discourage*. I looked up the meaning of the prefix *dis-*. I was surprised to learn that it meant "to take away," so to be *discouraged* means "to have courage taken out of you."[2] Not good. The good news is that the prefix *en-* means "to put into," so *encourage* means "to put courage into you."[3]

I love the word *encourage*, don't you? I need to be encouraged, and I know you do too. Did you know that the Holy Spirit's name in Greek is *paraklētos*, which can mean "advocate," "encourager," or "comforter"?[4] Isn't it amazing that God put this supernatural

Encourager inside you, inside me, to encourage us when we are discouraged?

In this chapter I want to share with you how you can be encouraged, especially when you are in pain or suffering personal loss. But the type of encouragement I'm talking about is not superficial human comfort but supernatural, divine encouragement—the kind only God can give.

God, Please Encourage Me!

We had only been on the mission field a couple of years, renting an old two-story gray cement house on the edge of an apple orchard outside Vienna, Austria. The beauty of the countryside thrilled my heart, but it couldn't erase the ache of being far, far away from my loved ones. And at no time was the pain of separation more piercing than that summer morning when I answered the phone and heard the voice of my brother, Tommy, who lived in California.

"Linda. Oh, Linda, a terrible accident. Angie pushed out the screen on the second-floor window and fell . . ."

No! My little three-year-old niece?

Between sobs, Tommy gulped out details. "Fell two flights . . . hit her head on cement . . . unconscious . . . the doctors, not sure . . . may never be normal."

"Oh, Tommy, Tommy. I'm sorry. I love you, brother. I love Angie. Oh, I'll be praying. I know God will be with Angie, even while she's unconscious. I know He will." By the time I hung up the phone, I was sobbing uncontrollably.

Tommy was my little brother—the one I fought for, the one I protected. When we were kids, he'd crawl into my bed and hide under my covers on nights when our father was uncontrollably drunk. This was his hiding place, where he felt safe. I'd hug him and calm his fears, telling him that everything would be okay. But how could I comfort him now with an ocean between us?

I went outside and walked through the apple trees, sobbing and praying. *God, You are Tommy's refuge and strength, an ever-present help in his time of need. Oh, God, I feel helpless to help. Let Your presence comfort them. Please God, please.*

I went up on the balcony outside our master bedroom overlooking the apple trees and just stood there and said, "God, God, God." When everyone was asleep that night, I went downstairs to the living room and bowed with my face on the floor. In the dark, with no words, I wept.

Then a warm softness enveloped me, like a blanket. A gentle hug, really. I knew God was holding me, pouring encouragement into me, just like I had when I used to hug Tommy and encourage him when he was little. God was my hiding place, my source of supernatural encouragement when nothing and no one else could comfort me. I was at peace—I knew He was holding Angie in His strong arms.

When we are walking through pain and loss, discouragement can threaten to overwhelm us.

How can you be encouraged even when things around you are falling apart?

Encouragement on the Spot

When pain comes your way, you need instant, on-the-spot encouragement. But how can you find it? I found the answer in a Bible verse years ago that so intrigued me that I wrote it in the front of my Bible. Let's take a look at this fascinating verse hidden in the middle of one of David's battles.

David's Source of Encouragement

David was in a crisis.

He and his six hundred mighty men had returned home to discover that the Amalekites had burned their town while they were away, stolen all their possessions, and kidnapped their wives and children.

The men wept and wailed in deep agony. Everything they cared about . . . gone!

Then their mood changed from grief to anger. This bitter anger flowed toward their leader: David. *This is all David's fault! If we hadn't followed him, this never would have happened.* The men picked up stones and surrounded David, ready to stone him to death.

That's when David did something unusual. He made a split-second decision.

> But David encouraged himself in the LORD his God.
> 1 SAMUEL 30:6, KJV

How did David do this? It was as if David momentarily suspended the drama around him and hid himself in the presence of God. In this safe place, God encouraged David.

David writes in Psalm 32:7, "You are my hiding place; you will protect me from trouble and surround me with songs of deliverance." As he communed with his God, God showed him a plan. David announced the plan to the angry men, and instead of stoning him, they followed him. They rescued their loved ones from the Amalekites and recovered all that had been stolen from them (1 Samuel 30:18-19).

David's Heart Journal

David knew how to encourage himself in the Lord because he'd had many, many years of practice. His training began as a shepherd boy. He sought God as he wandered through the hills with his flock. At night, he lay down on a mountainside and looked up at the stars—it was here that he began to know God as his creator. He discovered God to be his strength when he pulled a lamb from the mouth of a lion. He declared God to be his King when God gave him victory over the giant Goliath.

David recorded many ways he encouraged himself in the Lord in his heart journal. Oh, you didn't know that David kept a journal? He did! And we can peek inside his journal and see what he did, even though the details he shares are often so intimate and vulnerable that we fear we are invading his privacy. When we read the Psalms, we call them Scripture. But they weren't Scripture to David! David probably only had the Pentateuch, the first five books of the Bible.[5] These he studied and knew well! David had a deep love relationship with God that spilled over into the pages of our Bibles—at least seventy-five of the Psalms are actually the poetic writings of David that describe his prayers and pleas as he encountered various situations.

Let's flip through the pages of David's heart journal and look at four major ways David encouraged himself in the Lord: through (1) creation, (2) Scripture, (3) worship, and (4) a hiding place.

Creation

David loved the beauty and majesty of God's creation. Creation was alive. The trees clapped their hands; thunder roared God's voice. The fields danced for joy. David delighted in it all—it was as if he danced through creation worshiping God with a thankful heart. When he gazed at the heavens, he saw a story in the skies.

> The heavens proclaim the glory of God.
> The skies display his craftsmanship.
> Day after day they continue to speak;
> night after night they make him known.
> They speak without a sound or word;
> their voice is never heard.
> Yet their message has gone throughout the earth,
> and their words to all the world.
>
> PSALM 19:1-4, NLT

For me, pain is defused when I walk out in the glory of God's creation. I walk through fresh green grass, pick a wildflower, look up at the brilliant blue sky, and sigh. Problems melt away as the breeze blows over me and the quiet of the woods envelops me. I feel the same when I bundle up and trudge in newly fallen snow or run laughing through the rain. Somehow the world is at peace, and I'm able to center my heart on the God who created all this beauty. I start these walks in pain. When my walk ends, I realize that God has lifted my spirits and my perspective just by allowing me to experience His creation.

Scripture

I'm guessing that David carried a copy of Scripture in his knapsack along with his lunch when he took the sheep to the hills as a young man. Why do I think this? Because David loved God's Word, and it's obvious that he studied it with zeal. He wrote that God's Word restored his soul, made him wise, rejoiced his heart, and enlightened his eyes (Psalm 19:7-8). Look at further thoughts David wrote in his heart journal about how God's Word encouraged him.

The commandments of the Lord are right,
  bringing joy to the heart.
The commands of the Lord are clear,
  giving insight for living.
Reverence for the Lord is pure,
  lasting forever.
The laws of the Lord are true;
  each one is fair.
They are more desirable than gold,
  even the finest gold.
They are sweeter than honey,
  even honey dripping from the comb.
PSALM 19:8-10, NLT

Your word I have treasured in my heart,
That I may not sin against You.
PSALM 119:11, NASB

This is my comfort in my affliction,
That Your word has revived me and given me life.
PSALM 119:50, AMP

Open my eyes, that I may behold
Wonderful things from Your law.
PSALM 119:18, NASB

Can you feel David's eagerness to meditate on God's Word? It continually infused new life into him and revived his soul. What could be more encouraging than that?

Worship

David loved to write worship songs and love poems to the God he loved. He wrote his thoughts in good times and in hard times.

Consider when David's son Absalom was chasing him, trying to kill him and steal his throne. Can you imagine? Your own child, whom you love, is determined to take your life and the kingdom you rule? But because of David's deep intimacy with God, in this moment of crisis he wrote Psalm 63, which talks about how he delighted himself in God. Only someone whose heart is tightly tied to Yahweh can worship Him in such a devastating situation. Psalm 63 causes me to fall to my knees and say, *Give me a heart like David's in the good times and the painful times.*

David wrote Psalm 18 when the Lord rescued him from his many enemies, including King Saul, who resolved to kill him on many occasions. When David's life was at stake, instead of giving in to fear, he worshiped God as his hiding place.

> I love you, GOD—
>   you make me strong.
> GOD is bedrock under my feet,
>   the castle in which I live,
>   my rescuing knight.
> My God—the high crag
>   where I run for dear life,
>   hiding behind the boulders,
>   safe in the *granite hideout.*
> I sing to GOD, the Praise-Lofty,
>   and find myself safe and saved.
>
> PSALM 18:1-3, MSG (EMPHASIS ADDED)

Where did David go to write about Scripture, creation, and worship in his heart journal? He found a place to be alone with God, a hiding place.

A Hiding Place

Are you a little unclear what David means when he says that God is his hiding place? Let me offer a bit of explanation, because you, too, have a hiding place in God, and it's important for you to know how to access it.

Scripture makes it clear that God is our hiding place (Psalms 27:5; 32:7; 119:114). David's hiding place in God was a spiritual destination—a safe refuge where his mind, heart, and spirit went to be utterly alone with God. In this place David communed with his majestic God, spirit to Spirit, and God encouraged him.

How do you and I make God our hiding place? First, we prepare and ready our hearts. We ask the Holy Spirit to take us to a *spiritual destination*, a private refuge where we can talk with God like we talk face-to-face with our best friends. Second, we find a safe *physical location* that becomes a place for us to be with God. In Psalm 18 David calls his physical location a "granite hideout." Other times he hid in the cleft of a rock or sat by the waterfalls of En Gedi.

When the men were picking up the stones to kill David, he didn't have time to run to his granite hideout. He only had time to sink down into his spiritual destination—that private place where he received encouragement from the Holy Spirit.

My hiding place is a source of on-the-spot encouragement, but it's also a source of encouragement when I'm challenged year after year during a long struggle. Some friends of mine needed God's ongoing encouragement as they faced a struggle that continued with no end in sight.

Encouragement in the Long Struggle

Crystal and her husband, Doug, were living their dream as cowboy missionaries in Alaska. Doug was the horsemanship director at Victory Bible Camp, teaching lessons, leading trail rides, and caring for more than twenty-five horses. Crystal cared for their four sons, worked with the wranglers, and helped in the camp kitchen. Their sons were in boy heaven—mountains for their backyard, a small school, horses to ride, and wide-open spaces to explore.

Everything came to a screeching halt the day Doug had a supposedly not-difficult surgery on his brain. After that surgery, his brain worked fine, but his entire body had shut down. He lost his abilities to walk, speak, and eat. The family had to move to Kansas and learn a whole new way of living.

When Crystal describes her life, she pictures Doug and her as a lovely green vase. In Alaska, the vase overflowed with roses, tulips, and sunflowers. "We had purpose and a beautiful ministry that blessed others." But Doug's surgery punctured a huge hole in the vase. Other cracks appeared:

Moving from Alaska to Kansas . . . *CRACK!*

Financial strain due to medical bills and Doug's inability to work . . . *CRACK!*

Designing a wheelchair-accessible home to meet Doug's needs . . . *CRACK!*

Boys adjusting to a new community and school . . . *CRACK!*

Physical exhaustion of being on call 24/7 . . . *CRACK!*

Doug learning to live with many limitations . . . *CRACK!*

Their entire family suffered terribly. Crystal had many long talks with God. One went like this.

Crystal: *God, could You please, please smooth over these cracks and holes and make this vase usable again?*

God: *The cracks and holes are how I radiate through you. The holes make you holy.*

Crystal: *Okay. So I guess that's a no. Well then, could You please heal Doug just a little so he could have some form of normal function?*

God: *I have a different plan.*

Crystal: *Really? What could be better than healing him? That's what we want. Wouldn't that bring You glory?*

God: *Trust My plan.*

Crystal: *Okay, God. Your plan doesn't make sense to me. But if this is what will glorify You most, then Doug says yes. I say yes.*

What does Doug's yes look like?

Doug starts his day by listening to the Bible for an hour (he's on his twenty-second listening through the entire Bible since his surgery), and then he spends the rest of the morning hours praying for specific people. In the afternoon, Doug writes for one or two hours, using an app on his iPad that allows him to select one word at a time from a pop-up menu. Using this painfully slow process, he has written eight (yes—eight!) little books.

Doug's life is beyond hard. He can smell food, but he can't eat it. He has things to say, but he can't speak. His brain works great, but he can't communicate, even with the wife he loves. He longs for heaven every day, but he chooses to live God's purposes for his life while he is here. Crystal never dreamed that she would be a 24/7 caretaker for the man she loves. She takes him to the bathroom, gives him showers, puts food into his feeding tube every two hours, transfers him to each place that he needs to be, and talks for him. Does she weary of the routine? Of course! There have been times when she's wondered, *Why am I not completely falling apart? How am I still able to exist through this?* That, she believes, is God's grace. And because of that, both Doug and Crystal can have joy in the midst of the difficult journey.

I asked Crystal several questions to help me better understand how she finds encouragement from God in this long struggle:

How do you encourage yourself in the Lord?

> It's interesting—now that my old life has been taken from me, my time with Him has become more valuable and purposeful. I love God's Word. I feed on it—it's literally daily bread to my spirit. Each day I read from both the Old and New Testaments, and I am memorizing 1 John, which speaks of God's love for me. Also, I take a morning prayer walk each day for about an hour. This helps keep my body in shape, but it also keeps my spirit in shape because it's always a rich time with the Holy Spirit.

What do you do when the hardship of life overwhelms you?

> When I feel overwhelmed, I write each frustration on a piece of paper. Then I picture Jesus sitting in front of me with outstretched hands. I put the pieces of paper into His hands, and He says, "I've got this." Immediately the weight of worry lifts from my shoulders.
>
> Sometimes, though, I get so angry that instead of handing Jesus the scraps of paper, I wad them up and

throw them at Him. I feel like God has asked too much of me! But Jesus just sits there, calmly accepting whatever I bombard Him with. Then He tells me, "Crystal, let go and let Me have it all."

Crystal and Doug, if you could say anything to the people reading this book, what would you say?

Crystal: During those years when we lived as missionaries in Alaska, I felt like we were in the game. But God has been helping us see that in Alaska we were only on the sidelines preparing for the game—now we're in the game. In Alaska, our lives were about us and what we wanted. Breaking news here: It is not about you, and it is not about me. It's about what God wants to do in our lives. It's about how God wants to use us.

Doug: As my physical world has gotten smaller, God has gotten bigger. We try to fit God into our lives rather than make our lives fit into God. It's not about us; it's about God.[6]

Doug's response makes me think of Max Lucado's hard question: "Is there any chance, any possibility, that you have been selected to struggle for God's glory?"[7]

We don't want to answer that question, do we? But Doug and Crystal answered yes. They could have decided to believe that God had abandoned them and let them down. But instead they turned to God for encouragement in their long struggle. Because they've nestled down into God's plan for them, they are at peace. Crystal encourages herself in the Lord daily, and so does her dear Doug.

God is their hiding place. As Lucado writes, "Your faith in the face of suffering cranks up the volume of God's song."[8]

Encouragement Flows Forward

Jesus says, "If anyone is thirsty, let him come to Me and drink. He who believes in Me . . . 'From his innermost being will flow rivers of living water'" (John 7:38, NASB). When I look at my friends Crystal and Doug, I see the Holy Spirit flowing His living water to them and through them in a long, hard situation. But amazingly, these rivers now flow through them to many others. This is what receiving God's encouragement to us in our pain can do: We who are encouraged then become conduits of encouragement.

Recently Crystal shared this news: "Oh Linda, God is so good! He's given me two wonderful new opportunities. I'm now on staff with Thrive Ministry and mentoring women missionaries over Zoom. Also, Doug and I are speaking at women's retreats."

I asked, "How does Doug speak?"

Crystal laughed and said that while she did the speaking, Doug sat in his wheelchair in the back of the room and prayed—and when he wanted certain thoughts shared with the women, she'd put on a cowboy hat and speak as if she were her cowboy husband.

"Linda, I'm so glad that God is using our pain to encourage others," she said. "This encourages us!"

Isn't that what encouragement is all about? As we read in 2 Corinthians 1:3-4 (ESV),

> Blessed be the God and Father of our Lord Jesus Christ, the Father of mercies and God of all comfort, who comforts us in all our affliction, so that we may be able to

comfort those who are in any affliction, with the comfort with which we ourselves are comforted by God.

The words in David's heart journal have comforted millions down through the centuries! Martin Luther, the great Reformer, took great encouragement from Psalm 46. Look at these verses, which speak of encouragement and comfort:

God is our refuge and strength,
A very present help in trouble.
PSALM 46:1, NASB

"Be still, and know that I am God."
PSALM 46:10

As Martin Luther was preparing his Ninety-Five Theses, which would ultimately usher in the Protestant Reformation, he suffered greatly from depression. Whenever he was deeply discouraged, Luther would go to his friend and colleague Philip Melanchthon and say, "My friend, let's go sing the forty-sixth!"[9]

Singing Psalm 46 helped Luther hide himself in God during the trials he faced. In fact, he was so encouraged in his spirt that he wrote a majestic hymn around Psalm 46 that we still sing today: "A Mighty Fortress Is Our God."

Isn't the flow of encouragement amazing? God encouraged David to write Psalm 46, which encouraged Luther so much that he wrote a classic hymn based on it, and over five hundred years later, that hymn encourages me!

In 1 Thessalonians 5:11, the apostle Paul writes, "Encourage one another and build each other up." As followers of Jesus, we want to help others be stronger in their faith, even when life is challenging. I love how Larry Crabb and Dan Allender put it: "Verbal encouragement includes the idea of one person's joining someone else on a journey and speaking words that encourage the traveler to keep pressing on despite obstacles and fatigue."[10]

Why do you think Doug, even with his disabilities, has a life full of meaning and purpose? How has he been able to listen to the Bible twenty-two times and center in on praying for others? Because he has a wife who pours encouragement over him day after day. She literally lays down her life for him, just like Jesus did for us. That is love. Real love. Jesus love. True encouragement.

This is a hard world, so let me ask you a couple of hard questions: If you are married, who is going to breathe encouragement into your husband if you don't? A boss? Coworkers? Friends? I hope so. But God put you beside your mate to pour courage into him. Will you?

If you are a parent or grandparent, who is going to encourage your children—your grandchildren—if you don't? Teachers? Friends? Oh, I hope they will. But we have a special role. Our children and grandchildren live in a rapidly changing world. Our love, words, and encouragement give them strength to keep on keeping on. Will you take the time to pray, plan, and send a card or little gift to them?

No matter our role in life, each of us has been placed in community, friendships, and extended family where people are in desperate need of encouragement. Will you ask your God to show you anew what it looks like for you to be an encourager to those you love?

Hiding Myself in God

True encouragement to others cannot come from a place of emptiness. It must come from the overflow of abundance that the Holy

Spirit pours into me. That's why I run to my hiding place in God so often, asking the Holy Spirit to fill me up with supernatural encouragement.

I was in my late thirties when my sweet niece fell from that upper-story window, and I was just beginning to learn how to encourage myself in the Lord. Now I'm over eighty, and I'm still learning.

I still remember the day I cried out to my God, *Take me deeper in You, Father! I want more of You. You are God, and I am not. I'm through asking why. You are holy, You are other, and I bow before You. I want all of You.* I'd been a Christian for over thirty years. I was a missionary. I loved the Lord. But I knew I wanted—I *needed*—more. After placing that honest desire before God, something changed. It was as if God opened a door inside me and I went to a whole new level of experiencing His encouragement.

Have you cried out to God and told Him that you want to go deeper in Him? Have you told Him that you desire to love Him with all your heart, all your soul, all your mind, and every ounce of strength you have? Have you surrendered all to Him—your losses, your disappointments, your dreams—and told Him that you will trust Him, even if your life hasn't turned out quite like you want?

This morning I go to my hiding place, turn on Matt Redman's old song "Facedown," and fall on my knees, covering my face with my hands. The Spirit of God envelops me and pours encouragement into me. I love His presence. It encourages me like nothing else!

This is all that matters. Being with Him, the One I love. Every Heart Skill you have learned to this point will be nurtured in your hiding place. That's why this is so important—it's how you go deeper in loving and trusting God.

Heart Skill
A HIDING PLACE

Make God your hiding place.

1. In quiet solitude, ask the Holy Spirit to take you to a spiritual destination, a private refuge where you can talk with God face-to-face like you talk with a friend.

2. Find a safe physical location that becomes a place for you to meet regularly with your Beloved. The more time you spend in your hiding place, the easier it will become to find on-the-spot encouragement.

3. For creative ideas, see page 217 in the Bible study.

CHAPTER 8

PRAISE

God inhabits the praises of His people.
BASED ON PSALM 22:3, KJV

Praise

PRAISE

The fifty-seven-year-old man sighed as he sat in his chair, shoulders slumped, head hung.

Highly ambitious, he'd slipped from being revered in the highest social and political echelons of British society to being ignored by his adoring public. His last opera had been a failure; his opera company had gone bankrupt. His dreams were shattered. His hope was gone. Depression slipped its dark fingers around him and threatened to strangle him.

But then, a spark. An idea birthed from a collection of biblical excerpts from a minor poet.

He moved quickly from depression to obsession.

For twenty-four days he stayed in seclusion. He had little interest in food or sleep. The melodies in his head, the arpeggios blending and building, swooping and soaring. He was driven to capture it all on paper.

At times, he would jump up, wave his hands in the air, and shout, "Hallelujah!" Later he would tell others that during this intense time of composition, "I think I saw all heaven before me and the great God Himself."[1]

Who is this man? You know him. Well, maybe not personally, but you know his work.

Let the music rise in your mind. Hear the refrain: "Wonderful Counselor, the Mighty God, the Everlasting Father, the Prince . . . of . . . Peace."

The *Messiah* is George Frideric Handel's musical masterpiece, shouting hallelujah to the glory of God down through the centuries and around the entire world. Dozens of times the word *hallelujah* rings out. (*Hallal* [from *Halel*] means "praise," and *jah* [or *yah*] is a shortened form of *Yahweh*, the personal name of God.) With its blood-pulsing rhythm and layered building of orchestral voices, the Hallelujah Chorus is so masterful that it forces a physical response from the listener. At a performance of the *Messiah* in London, King George of England was so moved by the music that he stood in honor of God. That tradition continues to this day!

Like King George, I cannot sit when I hear the Hallelujah Chorus. I jump to my feet, raise my arms to the heavens, and shout, "Hallelujah!" My emotions are stirred, and my body follows in response. Like Handel, when I allow my grief and lament to move me toward God—as I experience His love, as I learn to trust and forgive and live encouraged—I find myself in the only posture that can sustain my heart through any circumstance or hurt. Praise is the final wisdom, the ultimate *hokmah*, of pain.

A Man Who Loved God

There is a book in the Bible that, much like the Hallelujah Chorus, stirs my emotions deeply enough to create a physical response in my body. When I read it, I don't stand and shout "Hallelujah"— I fall to my knees and weep. This, too, is a posture of praise.

What is this book? The book of Daniel. Most people think of Daniel as the one who was thrown into a lion's den and saved by God, who sewed shut the mouths of the lions. You may also remember Daniel as someone who had a special ability to interpret dreams or read handwriting on the wall. But there's so much more to Daniel. He was a man who worshiped his God even when everything in his life had been ripped from him. Daniel inspires me to praise God in the midst of my pain.

Last night, while watching the news with my husband, Jody, I was moved by a story of two young Ukrainians sharing about their time as Russian prisoners during the war between the two countries. They described how they were brainwashed, made to speak only the Russian language, isolated, and told that they must become Russians. They were put in solitary confinement or punished in other ways if they didn't sing the Russian national anthem.[2] I said to Jody, "This is just what happened to Daniel."

In the book of Daniel, we read the story of the Israelites taken into captivity in Babylon after the Babylonians utterly destroyed their country. Like those Ukrainian teenagers, Daniel was young—just sixteen or so—when he watched his parents, siblings, home, and country be destroyed. His future, his name, his culture, and his language were taken from him. Daniel and three of his friends were taken because they were of royal or noble birth and the Babylonians wanted to train them to become wise men for Babylon.

What does all this have to do with praise? The first six chapters of the book of Daniel are historical, and the last six are prophetic, but every time I read the book, I see worship. In many stories and passages, I notice the questions *To whom will Daniel bow? To whom will the kings bow?* And when I reach the end, I feel that I have read a love story between Daniel and his God.

I am awed by Daniel! How did Daniel worship God in unbearable circumstances? This is what God's Word shows us:

~ Daniel remembered his real name.
~ Daniel remembered who God is.
~ Daniel remembered his secret praise practice.

Daniel Remembered His Real Name

Daniel's Hebrew parents named him Daniel, which in Hebrew means "God is my judge" or "I am responsible to God, not people." Daniel's three friends also had special Hebrew names:

~ Hananiah: "The Lord is gracious."
~ Mishael: "Who (or what) is the Lord?"
~ Azariah: "The Lord is my help."

Holy names. Beautiful names wrapped in the love of Yahweh. But that, too, the Babylonians took from them, giving them new names that reflected their pagan culture:

- ∼ Daniel became Belteshazzar: "May Bel protect his life."
- ∼ Hananiah became Shadrach: "Command of Aku" (the moon god)
- ∼ Mishael became Meshach: "Who (or what) Aku is"
- ∼ Azariah became Abednego: "Servant of Nebo"[3]

Do you see, my friend? Before his captivity, every time someone spoke Daniel's name, or his friends' names, they were declaring praise to Yahweh, the true God. After captivity, every time someone spoke their names, the heathen gods of Babylon—Bel, Aku, and Nebo—received praise.

Daniel was taken captive around age sixteen and lived in captivity until he was at least eighty-three. But Daniel never forgot his given name. He lived "God is my judge" for sixty-seven years because he bowed only to Yahweh, not to the Babylonian gods or the heathen kings he served. Every time he was called Belteshazzar, Daniel remembered his true name. This is how he lived: "I am responsible to God, not man."

Daniel's choices cause me to ask, *Do my actions reflect my real name?* My parents didn't give me a name at birth that offers praise to God. Likely yours didn't either. But when you and I accepted Jesus, we were given the name Christian, which means "Christ follower." Oh, I want to be like Daniel, to be true to my name and follow the example of Jesus! *Help me hope like Jesus, love like Jesus, lament and trust and forgive like Jesus. Help me be true to my name.*

PRAISE

Daniel Remembered His God

When Daniel was eighteen and in the second year of the College of the Wise Men, the Babylonian king had a troubling dream. None of the king's wise men could identify the dream or interpret its meaning. In fact, they told the king that no man on earth could do both those things (Daniel 2:10). The king was so angered by this that he ordered all the wise men—including Daniel and his friends—to be killed. When Daniel heard of this, he requested time from the king so he "might declare the interpretation [of the dream] to the king" (Daniel 2:16, NASB). But what did Daniel do first?

> Daniel went to his house and informed his friends, Hananiah, Mishael and Azariah, about the matter, so that they might request compassion from the God of heaven concerning this mystery, so that Daniel and his friends would not be destroyed with the rest of the wise men of Babylon.
> DANIEL 2:17-18, NASB

Daniel was an exceptional young man. He led his friends in prayer to their compassionate God. Then he went to sleep, and God revealed the mystery of the king's dream to him in a night vision (Daniel 2:19). And, oh, the prayer that flowed from Daniel's lips!

> "Let the name of God be blessed forever and ever,
> For wisdom and power belong to Him.
> "It is He who changes the times and the epochs;
> He removes kings and establishes kings;

> He gives wisdom to wise men
> And knowledge to men of understanding.
> "It is He who reveals the profound and hidden things;
> He knows what is in the darkness,
> And the light dwells with Him.
> "To You, O God of my fathers, I give thanks and praise,
> For You have given me wisdom and power;
> Even now You have made known to me what we requested of You,
> For You have made known to us the king's matter."
> DANIEL 2:20-23, NASB

Daniel's prayer demonstrates that despite the mortal danger he was in, he knew exactly who God is. He spoke confidently of the wisdom of God, the sovereignty of God, the omniscience of God, the faithfulness of God.

Not only did God protect Daniel, but Daniel's confident praise of God led to more than he could have ever imagined. After this young captive correctly interpreted his dream, King Nebuchadnezzar promoted Daniel and made him ruler over the whole province of Babylon and chief prefect over all the wise men of Babylon (Daniel 2:48).

Daniel trusted God in the face of death, which enabled him to walk in peace. I read Daniel's words and ask God to help me do the same: *God, when I am in pain like Daniel, I want to trust You for divine insight that only You can give.*

Daniel Remembered His Praise Practice

We remember Daniel because of the miraculous events in his life, but the bulk of his everyday existence consisted of administrative decisions for a nation whose rulers had held him captive since he was a teenager. That meant that Daniel would have spent much of his life performing ordinary tasks without clear signs of God's love and intervention in his pain. Any of us who have experienced profound loss know how difficult that can be—wondering what God is up to, wondering if God cares, wondering if healing will ever come.

A psychologist would have looked at Daniel's background and said, "This man will have trauma reactions, abandonment issues, anger issues." But that's not what we see from Daniel in Scripture.

For the sixty-seven or so years of his captivity, Daniel had a secret that was a wellspring of thanksgiving for him, a catalyst of praise. We read of Daniel's secret in Daniel 6:10 (NASB):

> Daniel . . . entered his house (now in his roof chamber he had windows open toward Jerusalem); and he continued kneeling on his knees three times a day, praying and giving thanks before his God, as he had been doing previously.

Daniel devoted time each day in secret to be alone with his holy God. Not once a day, but three times a day. Whether God intervened in his pain or not, Daniel persisted in praise. Because Daniel met his Father God on his knees three times a day, every day, God's perspective on life became Daniel's perspective. God's worldview became his. Even when Daniel was over eighty years old and it probably pained him to get on the floor, he did it! He'd been meeting his God three times every day for sixty-seven years.

I can tell you this as someone who has also been on my knees before God over decades through many kinds of deep suffering: The experience of God's presence and faithfulness changes us. It accumulates in our hearts and souls over time. Praise becomes our natural language because we cannot live without it.

This habit sustained Daniel over the long years, but that wasn't its only purpose. Regularly giving thanks before God continually aligned his heart with God's heart and prepared him to be battle ready when God moved. This secret history with God healed his wounds and formed him into a man of spiritual steel.

When certain Babylonian men jealously plotted against him, Daniel's heart and mind were prepared. These evil men knew that Daniel prayed to God three times a day, and they convinced the king to decree that people could pray to no other god or human but the king (Daniel 6:5-9).

And so, shortly after the decree, the evil men burst into Daniel's home and found him bowing in prayer to his God. *We've got him now!* they thought.

The pagan king realized that he had been tricked by the evil men. He respected Daniel and didn't want him to die. As Daniel was thrown into a lion's den in accordance with the decree, the king called out, "Your God whom you constantly serve will Himself deliver you" (Daniel 6:16, NASB).

Early the next morning, the king called down into the lion's den: "Daniel, servant of the living God, has your God, whom you constantly serve, been able to deliver you from the lions?" (Daniel 6:20, NASB).

Yes! Daniel's faithful God had delivered him!

Do you see why I want to be like Daniel? His commitment to praise God, even in the face of death, inspires me. His determination to be faithful to God—even when his nation, his culture, and his loved ones had been stripped from him—stirs fresh faith in me. His love for God and eruption of praise through his prayers propel me to my knees in thanksgiving to the almighty God. All was from God, through God, and for God.

PRAISE

A Modern-Day Daniel

I want you to get to know my dear friend Valerie, whom I call a modern-day Daniel. You'll see why as you learn more about her.

When I met Valerie twenty-five years ago, her children were two, four, six, and eight, and she was training for her fifth marathon. This was an athletic family! I remember the first time I walked into her master bedroom and came face-to-face with a huge climbing wall. (One of her children became a world-class rock climber.)

Valerie is so proud of her Native heritage—her Lakota grandfather was the first American Indian to serve in the United States Congress—that she gave all four of her children Indigenous names: Chancencia, Alishaunia, Tayanita, and Nakoa.

The indominable spirit Valerie inherited from her grandfather propelled her on even when the title *athlete* was stripped from her.

Before Valerie could run her fifth marathon, her body betrayed her. No one could diagnose what was wrong. Valerie wore maternity clothes for several years—not because she was pregnant but because of an abdominal distention. She's suffered eleven major surgeries. I remember visiting Valerie when she hadn't been able to walk down the stairs to her children's rooms for eight months. It hurt my heart. I said, "Valerie, how do you do this?"

Today, Valerie lives with a partial digestive system and is held together inside by a skin graft and web of scar tissue. She has very limited food choices.

But Valerie is a woman of praise. Her frail, unreliable body houses a fierce, indominable spirit intent on honoring God with her every breath. The faith with which my dear friend lives has encouraged me many times.

One day I asked Valerie if I could learn more about her lifestyle of praise. As we sat at my dining table, she told me, "Linda, I need to tell you up front that I'm uncomfortable with you comparing me to Daniel. Don't compare me to a spiritual giant. I struggle daily to trust God. I fail . . . often!"

"I won't, Valerie, I promise," I said. "But names are important to you, right? And, like Daniel, you were stripped of your identity through much suffering?"

She laughed. "Linda, enough! You promised . . ."

"Okay, okay. I'm not saying you're perfect—none of us are. I'm only trying to show that themes of faithfulness like Daniel's guide your own life. Daniel's story opens with him being stripped of his identity. Let's start by talking about how this has been true for you as well. When I first met you, you would have identified yourself as an athlete. But your body had different plans."

"Yes," she agreed. "But my identity isn't based on what my body can or can't do. My identity is based on my relationship with Jesus. His Word declares who I am, and I'm believing His Word and not what the world and other people say or think."

"Your health struggles have been going on for decades, but something happened recently that further stripped you of your identity."

Valerie sighed. "I assume you're referring to my husband, who left me after almost forty years of marriage for a younger woman with the athletic health I have lost. He threw aside our 'until death do us part' vows and betrayed, rejected, and despised me."

"Valerie, my heart breaks over the deep pain this has caused my friend. You were childhood sweethearts; he gave you a ring when you were twelve that you'd always worn. You raised four children together. And now, because of his choices, you are divorced."

"I watched you work hard on your marriage and family," I told her. "You never wanted this pain—to see your family torn apart."

"It's true," she said. "But in my journey of praising God, I've experienced how praise and pain can coexist."

"You know a lot about pain. In fact, you've experienced something you call 'I-can't-breathe pain.' What is that?"

"Well, it is how it sounds," she told me. "Pain that is so hardcore and gut-wrenching that you sometimes feel like you can't breathe and you tell God to let you die. I felt that kind of pain on a physical level with most all my surgeries. But to feel that pain on an emotional level is even harder. Betrayal hits hard. Rejection delivers a hurtful punch. And, added to that, one of my daughters personalized my health trauma to the point that she attempted suicide. My mama heart was ripped to shreds. I couldn't help her. I felt responsible for her despair. I fell to the ground sobbing, pleading, and screaming, 'No! No! No!' Then I pleaded and screamed again. I kept fighting the fear in me and releasing her into the arms of God. At one point, God whispered, *Valerie, I have her. I'm holding her. I am with her right now. Trust Me.*"

Valerie tucked a strand of her shoulder-length black hair behind her ear, and I asked, "Yet you continued to trust God and to praise Him despite your pain. How is that even possible? Wait, I see that smile! It has to do with your secret practice, doesn't it?"

Valerie nodded.

"You and Daniel both had secret habits that you practiced three times a day for decades. What's the special thing you do?"

"My secret practice is reciting one hundred names of God," Valerie shared. "There are many names of God throughout the Bible, but about twenty years ago, I began memorizing a few names and speaking them out loud. I started alphabetically and added new names over time.

"'He is the Almighty. He is the Bread of Life. He is the Creator of all things. He is the Everlasting Father.' Each time I spoke one of God's names, an almost imperceptible authority surged through me, a power that was not mine but that was in me and given to me. I felt God's life force strengthen my spirit. I memorized fifty names. Later on, I added another fifty." (You can find Valerie's "100 Names of God" on the facing page.)

"How often do you declare these names?" I asked her.

"I declare them every morning when I wake up. Also every night when I go to sleep. And I recite them in the middle of the day when I face hard things. There is power in declaring His names. His Spirit refreshes my soul with each name I speak."

I looked into Valerie's guileless eyes and nodded for her to continue.

"These hundred names of God do not encompass all that He is—God is always more than can be put into words. Yet I am embraced and hugged and loved as I praise God by speaking His names back to Him. It's personal. As God and I hold hands, I recite the many wonders of who He is. God not only authored His names—He continues to fulfill the promise that each name proclaims."

"Speaking His names excites you, doesn't it?"

"It does!" she said. "There's so much joy in these sacred moments. I have a heart-pounding awe knowing God is profoundly excited to greet me each day. His morning invitation is this: *Valerie, rise up and humbly follow Me as I reveal Myself to you today.* At night, another invitation whispers, *Do not worry. I do not slumber, but I will hold you while you do.* The habit is the same, and while the words I hear sometimes change, the invitation is always to trust Him."

I took the list she handed me and scanned through it.

"Every name of God calls me to rest in Him," she shared. "Every name of God tells me that I am held. Every name tells me

VALERIE'S 100 NAMES OF GOD

A
Alpha and Omega. Author of Faith. Abba. Advocate. Anointed One. Ancient of Days. Author of Salvation.

B
Banner of the Nations. Bishop of Our Souls. Branch of Righteousness. Bridegroom. Bread of Life. Bright Morning Star.

C
Chief Cornerstone. Commander. Consuming Fire. Crown of Glory. Christ. Creator of All Things.

D
Deliverer.

E
Elohim. El Shaddai. Emmanuel. Everlasting Father.

F
Faithful Witness. Father of Mercies. Fortress. Friend.

G
God of All Grace. God of Recompense. God of Patience and Comfort. Good Shepherd. Great High Priest.

H
Habitation of Justice. Healer. Help of My Countenance. He Who Will Come. Hiding Place. High and Lofty One. Husband. Holy One. Holy Spirit.

I
I Am.

J
Jesus Christ. Judge.

K
King of Kings.

L
Life-Giving Spirit. Living Stone. Lord of Hosts. Lamb of God. Light of the World. Lion of Judah. Lord of Lords. Love.

M
Man of Sorrows. Messenger of the Covenant. My Portion. Master. Mediator. Messiah. Mighty One.

O
Omnipotent. Omnipresent. Omniscient. Our Passover. Our Potter.

P
Paraclete. Precious Stone. Propitiation for Our Sins. Position. Prince of Peace. Purifier.

R
Rain upon the Mown Grass. Ransom. Refuge. Restorer. Ruler over Kings. Redeemer. Resting Place. Resurrection and the Life. Rock.

S
Sanctuary. Savior. Servant. Shadow of Great Spirit of Knowledge. Strength of My Life. Strong Tower. Sure Foundation.

T
Teacher. The Way. The Truth. The Life.

V
Vine. Voice of Yahweh.

W
Wisdom. Wonderful Counselor. Word of Life.

Y
Your Confidence. Your Keeper. Your Exceedingly Great Reward.

that I am loved. Every name declares that I can trust Him. Need there be any reason not to praise God? Even pain and suffering cannot hold back the floodgates of my praise, because nothing will be able to separate me from the love of God that is mine in Christ Jesus."

Valerie taught me about the power of speaking the names of the Father, Son, and Spirit. So now I also have the holy habit of speaking the names of God. No, I haven't memorized one hundred names like Valerie—my brain doesn't work as well as hers—but I can go through the alphabet once and declare at least ten of His names to Him every day. And I have my Name Tree to help me. After my daughter Joy died, Valerie made me a tree with the hundred names of God attached to it in creative ways. It hangs on the wall next to the ottoman where I kneel and worship my Beloved. I count my Name Tree among my most special possessions.

Praise is a Heart Skill that helped Daniel and Valerie find peace during the hardest times of their lives. You will also want to learn this secret practice so that your hallelujahs to God can become clearer and louder with each passing year of your life.

A Song of Praise

What a joy it's been for me to journey with you from hope to praise. I said at the beginning of this book that I wanted to teach you eight Heart Skills, eight interlocking practices to strengthen you during hard times so you can live life with your God as a thing of beauty. I hope you find these Heart Skills useful tools that you will use the rest of your life. And I hope you glimpse the *hokmah* wisdom buried beneath each Scripture you pondered and each story that unfolded. I also pray that you heard the song behind the words.

Listen! The music calls to you now.

Hope sings her song of new possibility. She joins hands with Love, whose rich contralto harmony boldly proclaims that God's love will get you through any loss, no matter how painful. Next come Loss and Lament. They sing in a minor key, giving voice to your pain. Lament reaches for the hand of Trust, who picks up the tempo of the song. Trust holds the hand of Forgiveness, who joins the refrain with a soaring song of freedom. Forgiveness grasps the hand of Encouragement, who hits a transcendent note that pierces through every cloud of despair.

The final voice to join the octet is Praise. She leads the melody now, but her voice has been humming underneath all along. You may not have noticed her resonant tone in the background when Hope first sang, but she was there. Without her, each voice is disconnected, lifeless. Praise holds all of them together, drawing them into a grand finale, a resounding crescendo of hallelujah to God. Hallelujah, hallelujah! A thousand hallelujahs to our God, who journeys with us in the hard times, who tenderly holds our hearts, who strengthens our faith, and who gives us the courage to face hard moments.

Lift your voice and sing! Hallelujah to the mighty Creator who holds the planets in their orbits and the seas in their boundaries. Hallelujah to the sovereign King, the Prince of Peace, the Messiah, the Word of Life. Hallelujah to our Healer, our Provider, our Guide. *Holy God, we sing praise to You, the one true God. To You be the glory forever and ever. Amen.*

Heart Skill
A PRACTICE

Begin your own holy habit of praising God daily. Spend some time alone with God and ask Him what names of His have been important to you over the years. Look at Valerie's list. Then select seven to ten different names of God, and praise Him with these names out loud every day.

YOUR EIGHT HEART SKILLS

Chapter	Heart Skill	Method
Hope	a declaration	a statement/symbol/decree that expresses your hope in God
Love	a plan	a spiritual workout plan designed to deepen your intimacy with God
Loss	a journal	daily writing in a Thankful Journal to help maintain perspective about your loss
Lament	a lament	a written prayer that expresses your sorrow to God
Trust	a verse (or verses)	a life verse or passage that expresses your trust in God
Forgive	a lifestyle	a choice not to keep a record of wrongs
Encourage	a hiding place	finding your spiritual and physical hiding place in God
Praise	a practice	a daily praise practice of declaring the names of God

EIGHT-WEEK BIBLE STUDY

Dear friend,

Welcome to the next eight weeks—they can literally be life-changing! I am excited about what God is going to do in your life as you dive into God's Word. It is good to read a book or go to a retreat and hear messages, but it's even better when you sink down into Scripture and let God Himself teach you.

In addition to studying God's Word and answering questions, each week you will complete a project called a Heart Skill. You will find each Heart Skill at the beginning of the lesson. Please read it first, because you will need time to ponder, pray, and then ponder some more as you ask God for His guidance. There is no right or wrong way to do these projects—you are developing a skill to breathe hope into you as God heals your hurting heart.

These eight Heart Skills have given me the tools I've needed to walk through pain and broken dreams. You will begin with hope—oh, blessed hope! Love will enable you to journey into loss and lament. These hard seasons lead you to trust, which enables you to forgive and move forward from your pain to encourage and praise. Even our pain can become not only a blessed but also an exciting journey. I'm so grateful you are joining me.

God the Father, Son, and Spirit is waiting to meet you in His Word! Know that I am praying for you!

Linda

EIGHT-WEEK BIBLE STUDY

Dear leader,

Thank you for guiding a group through this study. These chapters and the accompanying Bible studies are powerful, and I believe you will see the Lord work in mighty ways in your group.
    This is what Mindy King saw in her group:

> Life is hard. And learning to grieve the losses of life well is a skill we get to practice again and again. This study guides us in the forgotten art of lament and equips us with the Heart Skills we need to walk through the deepest valleys. Not only will you be encouraged to place your hope in the One who never fails, but you will also begin to see Him transform your pain into shouts of praise.

Give yourself time to dig deep into these chapters and to complete the weekly Heart Skills, and encourage your group to do the same! It's helpful to read the chapter and begin thinking about the accompanying Heart Skill early in the week so you have time to ponder and pray and allow the Lord to speak through the process. This study is dense, and you and your group members probably won't glean the depth of its riches in one go-round. Expect that there may be weeks when you or your group may feel behind. That's okay. Trust the Spirit's guidance. It's not the work we do that ultimately matters but the work He does in us. And He promises that He will be faithful to complete it!

God's blessings as you lead!
Linda

WEEK 1

Hope

Heart Skill
A DECLARATION

Ask the Holy Spirit to help you create your own Declaration of Hope (time: fifteen minutes to an hour). Your declaration can take any form: words based around a Scripture, a song, or a prayer. Plus you may want to draw a symbol or paint a picture. Be creative! The point is to have something concrete that grounds you in God's hope and that you can refer to again and again. Consider sharing your Declaration of Hope with your group.

1. Write your own Declaration of Hope.

My Hope Slide

2. Could you relate to my hope slide on page 8? When you consider the hard things before you, where would you put yourself on that slide (doubt, discouragement, despair, depression)?

3. Read 2 Corinthians 4:8-18.

    a. In verses 8-9, Paul is slipping down a slide but hasn't reached the bottom. Read these verses out loud before God. What hope do these words give you in light of your hard situation?

b. In these verses, Paul lists many reasons he doesn't lose heart. Make a list of or write a paragraph about what encourages you from these verses not to lose heart. Particularly note verse 18 (this verse was key for Paul).

My First Lesson in Hope

4. Reflect on what we learned about hope based on Romans 8:24-25.

   a. What stands out to you in these verses? What encouragement do they provide?

b. What has God taught you personally about hope? If you are willing, share with the group.

The Word of God Gives Me Hope
   5. Read Romans 15:4. What does this verse say to you about the Word of God?

6. Read Lamentations 3:21. What is the most challenging situation on your heart? Write a paragraph about what it looks like for you to dare to hope in this circumstance.

7. Read Lamentations 3:22-24. Paraphrase these verses as a prayer to God, thanking Him for who He is.

8. Think about your difficult situation. Write down three to five mercies, however small, that God has given you (maybe unexpected kindnesses, positive changes in your thinking, new resolves, or even new things you've seen about God).

9. Are there particular verses from God's Word that have infused you with hope? Write any here and be prepared to share them with your group.

The Spirit of God Gives Me Hope

10. On a scale of 1 to 10, with 1 being *not intimate* and 10 being *very intimate*, how would you describe your relationship with the Holy Spirit?

1   2   3   4   5   6   7   8   9   10

   a. How often do you talk with the Holy Spirit? When you talk with the Holy Spirit, are you able to be honest about your emotions?

   b. What might you do to draw closer to the Holy Spirit?

11. Several of the Holy Spirit's roles are mentioned in the chapter on page 16: comforter, helper, counselor, encourager. Look up these verses and list some of the Holy Spirit's other roles.

    John 14:26

    Romans 8:26

12. Romans 8:26 says that the Holy Spirit prays for you when you are in deep distress. Have you ever experienced this? If so, what did you feel? Write a prayer thanking the Holy Spirit for praying for you in this way.

13. Read John 14:16-17. Note where the Holy Spirit lives and how long He will live there.

    a. Have you ever thanked the Holy Spirit for choosing you to be His home? Why or why not?

    b. What holy work do you think the Holy Spirit wants to do through you in the coming weeks?

My Declaration of Hope

14. My Declaration of Hope included 2 Corinthians 1:3-4. Paraphrase these verses as a prayer to your God of comfort, who loves you, and ask Him to flood your heart with hope!

Hope Playlist

~ "New Wine" by Hillsong Worship
~ "Hope Has a Name" by River Valley Worship
~ "The Steadfast Love of the Lord" by Dave Hunt

WEEK 2

Love

Heart Skill
A PLAN

Spend time with God creating your own spiritual workout plan to help you grow in loving Him with all your heart, soul, mind, and strength (time: fifteen minutes to an hour). Review Linda's, Alix's, and Kim and Tracy's plans for ideas.

1. Write down your spiritual workout plan here. Consider sharing your Heart Skill with the group.

God's Love? Experience It!

2. Do you really understand just how much God loves you? That His heart delights in you and that He smiles at the very thought of you? Take some time and prayerfully soak in the following verses. Let the words wash over you and drench you with God's love, and then write down what aspects of God's love are most meaningful to you right now.

Psalm 23

Isaiah 43:1-4

Psalm 131

Isaiah 41:10

1 Corinthians 13:4-8

3. Read Romans 8:38-39 and my paraphrase of it on page 27. Write your own paraphrase of the verses here, applying them to your difficult situation.

4. The ladies in the Adoration Gals Bible study (see pages 29–30) each wrote a short paragraph about the ways they receive God's love. Write your own paragraph about how it looks for you to receive His love. Be sure to express how God's love changes the condition of your heart.

Becoming a Lover of God: Let's Learn!

Read Psalm 139 s-l-o-w-l-y and ponder David's love letter to God.

5. Write your own love letter to God, using Psalm 139 as an example of the kinds of things you might express to Him. If your love level with God isn't as passionate as David's, then write a letter to God honestly expressing where you are and where you want to be—maybe something like this:

> *Dear God, I can't imagine writing a letter like David's to You . . . It's just so personal. Help me be more personal with You.*

6. Read Luke 10:27. Juli loved God with her mind, soul, and strength, but she struggled to love Him with all her heart (see page 33). Of these four ways to love God, which comes most naturally to you? Which is the hardest? Write a prayer expressing your desire to become a lover of God with all your being.

Becoming a Lover of Others: Let's Learn!

7. Read Luke 10:30-37, the parable of the Good Samaritan. What does a modern-day Good Samaritan look like to you? Share an example with your group.

8. Has someone ever shown you practical and merciful love like Lorraine and Valerie showed me (sticky notes, flowers, and food)? Share with the group how these people blessed you.

9. People often avoid those in great pain because they don't know what to say (or they feel like they need to come up with something profound or spiritual). How does it free you up to know that comforting someone in pain can be a simple "I'm sorry" or just sitting beside them as they grieve? Who in your life needs this kind of love right now?

10. Read John 13:34-35. Jesus gave us a new commandment. Describe what this commandment means to you.

11. Brainstorm practical ways to show love to others in pain. I'll give you an idea to start!

    a. *Keep a playlist of worship songs to send to hurting people.*

    b.

    c.

    d.

    e.

    f.

12. The chapter began talking about the Adoration Gals and ended with the Elephant Herd.

    a. Why are groups of women committed to studying God's Word together and encouraging one another so important?

    b. Do you have an Elephant Herd to encourage you? If not, ask God to reveal where you can discover a group who fits you.

Love Playlist

~ "Just Be Held" by Casting Crowns
~ "Reckless Love" by Cory Asbury

WEEK 3

Loss

Heart Skill
A JOURNAL

Keep a Thankful Journal. It's easy to become myopic and consumed with loss during a painful time. This journal will help you keep a balanced perspective between what you suffer and your many blessings. For the next week, write at least three to five things a day for which you are thankful.

1. God understands that it's hard to thank Him when you are in the middle of difficult things. That's why the Bible calls this a "sacrifice of thanksgiving." Read Psalm 50:14 and Psalm 50:23. Write a prayer, a sacrifice of thanksgiving to God, about the hardest situation in your life.

2. Fill out the chart below. This will help you balance the blessings in your life with what you suffer as you begin writing in your Thankful Journal.

What I Have	What I Suffer

3. Share a few things you wrote in your Thankful Journal with your group.

Do I Accept My Loss?

As you answer the following questions, please respond in light of the most painful loss you currently face or have endured in the past. Prayerfully ask the Lord to give you new insights.

4. God showed me that He wanted me weak so I would rely on His strength rather than my own strength. Read 2 Corinthians 12:8-10.

    a. How do you view weakness? Why?

    b. Can you delight in weakness, or do you merely tolerate it?

    c. What does it mean that when you are weak, you are strong?

5. Get ready! This is a time for some soul-searching self-evaluation. Be brutally honest with yourself as you answer these three questions.

   a. What are some practical ways I've emotionally grieved the pain of my loss?

   b. How have I grieved the *scope* of my loss—the extent to which it's affected both me and others?

c. How has this loss changed how I view myself? How has this loss changed how others see me?

Your honest answers to these questions will reveal where you are in your healing journey. Stop now and pray. Thank God for what He has done and ask Him to help you move forward in this process.

How Does God Use Loss to Change Me?

6. Read James 1:2, the "toughest verse in the Bible." How have you been able to express joy during your loss? Does it help to know that you express joy *in* the loss rather than *for* the loss?

7. Think of someone you know who has demonstrated joy during a difficult trial. Write this person's name below and, if God should lead, share about this person with your group. Perhaps you'd like to write them a text or send them a card this week thanking them for their example to you.

8. Read James 1:3-4, the "fattest promise" in the Bible. The reason you can have joy in your loss is because, as you endure in faith, God releases transforming power in you so that you might be mature and complete, lacking nothing.

   a. When you feel like giving up, what helps you endure?

b. Endurance produces the fruit of the Spirit (Galatians 5:22-23). Which of these fruits do you see growing in your life?

Imagine your loss as a lane in a marathon race you are called to run. Lift your eyes. Something awaits you at the finish line. Do you see it? James calls it the crown of life. This crown is a reward given to those who persevere through trial, persecution, and painful situations with an enduring faith in God (James 1:12; Revelation 2:10).

9. How does the idea that a crown awaits you encourage you to press on?

10. Zane Hodges says in his commentary on James that this crown also refers to enrichment in our temporal experience here on earth (see his comment on page 56). How might pursuing this crown enrich you?

Endurance Hall of Fame

11. I shared three different people I would nominate to my personal Endurance Hall of Fame. Whom would you nominate, and why?

Loss Playlist

~ "Tell Your Heart to Beat Again" by Danny Gokey
~ "The Detour" by FAITHFUL
~ "It Is Well" by Kristene DiMarco (Bethel Music)

EIGHT-WEEK BIBLE STUDY

WEEK 4

Lament

Heart Skill
A LAMENT

Lament is a Heart Skill you'll use throughout your life. It's important to understand that lament is a process that God approves of and a way in which He heals you. Please read Psalm 77 in two different Bible translations. Then go through the three action steps to create your own lament:

> Cry out your complaint.
> Choose to remember.
> Worship God in His majesty.

Your Heart Skill: Write a Lament

1. *Cry out your complaint* (Psalm 77:1-10). Like Asaph, write your complaints. Be honest. (Refer also to Heidi's lament on pages 74–75 for an example.) Ask God direct questions and cry out your emotions. Your loving Father wants you to express your pain before Him.

2. *Choose to remember* (Psalm 77:11-12). Write what you choose to remember. (See my examples on pages 72–73.) For Asaph, crying out to God was an act of faith. Once all his complaints were expelled, he paused. His heart changed directions, and he chose to remember what he believed. Asaph's choice to remember moves his heart from hopeless to hopeful! He writes:

~ *I will remember*—the deeds of the Lord.
~ *I will remember*—the wonders of God.
~ *I will remember*—Your work and meditate on Your deeds.

I remember:

I remember:

3. *Worship God in His majesty* (Psalm 77:13-14). Add a paragraph to your lament that worships God in His majesty. (For extra inspiration, read Isaiah 6:1-5 and Revelation 4:9-11.)

Consider sharing your lament with your group.

4. To lament is Christian. It is how we bring our sorrow to God. Without lament, we're unsure how to process our pain. Which of these four ideas about lament on page 64 intrigues you most, and why?

    ~ a language for loss
    ~ a solution for silence
    ~ a framework for feelings
    ~ a process for our pain

5. Growing up, how did your family, church, or community process deep sorrow or death? Write examples.

6. Could you identify with any of the illustrations or stories under the section "The Disappearance of Lament" (page 65–68)?

7. Can you describe a time when you were in so much pain that you found it difficult to pray? What did you do?

8. What verses do you use to bring comfort to your soul when you are in pain or to help a friend in pain?

The Surprise of Lament

9. Did anything in this chapter surprise you?

10. Lament releases pain, but it doesn't allow you to stay in pain. Lament is designed to sweetly move you forward to hope and greater trust in God. Write a few sentences thanking God that hope and greater trust are in your future!

11. How has your understanding and appreciation of lament changed by reading this chapter, doing the Bible study, and writing your own lament?

Lament Playlist

~ "Son of Suffering" by Matt Redman
~ "He Loves You More" by Shannon Adducci

WEEK 5

Trust

Heart Skill
A VERSE

Ask God to show you a personal Trust Verse (or Trust Verses) that can encourage you today and guide you as you seek to trust Him in the coming years. Memorize this passage. Say it often. As you do, allow the power of God's Word to refresh and to strengthen your faith.

The Power of a Trust Verse

Other women who went through this study gave examples of their Trust Verses and how their verses encourage them. I hope their examples help you as you find your own Trust Verse.

Meagan

> Even though I walk through the valley of the shadow of death,
>   I will fear no evil,
> for you are with me;
>   your rod and your staff,
>   they comfort me.
>
> PSALM 23:4, ESV

Even though I walk through _____, You are with me. I fill in the blank with any- and everything. *Even though I walk through so much unknown and uncertainty, You are with me! Even though I walk through deep pain in my relationships, You are with me!* This is the verse I use to steady my heart, mind, and emotions during times of unknown, fear, or darkness.

Diane

Trust in the LORD with all your heart
And do not lean on your own understanding.
In all your ways acknowledge Him,
And He will make your paths straight.
PROVERBS 3:5-6, NASB

Because I am a professional counselor, people relay their stories of pain and trauma to me. I love them. I hurt when they hurt. In my profession, it's called *vicarious trauma* to sit with someone's trauma and feel the inner world of another while trusting God to lead and direct us both on the healing journey. *God created and loves this person, He alone knows the path of healing for this individual, and He is trustworthy in the journey.* I don't look to myself for wisdom. I look to Him. The only way I can do my job or be a loving wife, mother, or Grammi is to be completely dependent on Him.

Lorraine

We fix our eyes not on what is seen, but on what is unseen, since what is seen is temporary, but what is unseen is eternal.
2 CORINTHIANS 4:18

When I was a media-relations manager for a Fortune 200 company, the stress of leadership's expectations sometimes threatened to overwhelm me. Other situations also made me anxious—when our bank balance was lower than incoming bills, or when I had to make a decision that would change the trajectory of our family. In these moments I'd remember the promise in my Trust Verse and tell myself, *Lorraine, stop looking at what you see and focus instead on the One you can't see. God will get you through this, and He will accomplish eternal purposes in this temporary situation.* This thought always gave me peace and the perspective shift I needed.

1. How did reading these three examples help you understand the power of a Trust Verse?

2. Write your Trust Verse(s) here.

My Teacher of Trust

Begin by reading the book of Habakkuk (it's only three chapters!).

3. Habakkuk chose to trust God even when God's answer made no sense to him. Think of a time you trusted God when it made no sense to you. What did you learn during this time?

4. When God answered Habakkuk's prayer in a way that deeply troubled him, he ultimately said, "I will take my stand at my watchpost" (Habakkuk 2:1, ESV) to wait and see what would happen. He chose to *retreat, remember,* and *recommit* (see pages 88–89) as he waited. How did these three actions help strengthen Habakkuk's faith? How would choosing to retreat, remember, and recommit help you?

5. Habakkuk moved from doubt and lament in chapter 1 to worship and his beautiful statement of trust in Habakkuk 3:17-19. Using Habakkuk's words as a pattern, write your own list of *even though*s.

Even though _____,
I will _____.

Even though _____,
I will _____.

Even though _____,
I will _____.

Expressions of Trust

6. Read Laura's story on pages 92–93. Laura stopped asking *Why, God?* and began asking *How, God?* Think about the circumstances in your life and answer Laura's four *how* questions:

    a. How might God use your current trial to glorify Him?

b. How might God use your weakness, infirmity, or disability to display His power?

c. How might God use your hard circumstances to show you something about Him—or you?

d. How might God make your mess into a message?

7. Read Gary's prayer of surrender on page 94. He said, in essence, *I want whatever will glorify You most.* What does it look like for you to say this in your current circumstances? Write a paragraph.

8. Read Jeremiah 17:5-8. What does God promise that a person of trust can have even in a year of pain and drought?

EIGHT-WEEK BIBLE STUDY

9. Read how Alaine renewed her mind (pages 95–96). Her old mind was filled with horrid memories of the evil abuse done to her, but memorizing Scripture transformed her mind into a worship sanctuary for God. What Scripture have you memorized? How has memorizing Scripture changed the way you think? If you haven't yet memorized Scripture, what is one verse you could start with?

10. Alaine waited for over twenty years for God to answer her *why* question. How does His answer to her encourage you?

11. Read Psalm 131. What does the psalmist do with his unanswered questions?

12. Isaiah 26:3 is a beautiful Trust Verse that links peace, trust, and our thoughts: "You will keep in perfect peace all who trust in you, all whose thoughts are fixed on you!" (NLT). Write at least three ways you can fix your thoughts on the Lord this week.

13. Develop a list of your favorite go-to Trust Verses, songs, and quotes. Keep it on your phone, in your purse—somewhere you can find it on not-good trust days.

Trust Playlist

~ "Oceans (Where Feet May Fail)" by Hillsong UNITED
~ "Blessings" by Laura Story

WEEK 6

Forgive

Heart Skill
A LIFESTYLE

First Corinthians 13:5 says that love "keeps no record of wrongs." Memorize this verse, and write today's date next to it in your Bible. Your Heart Skill is to choose *today*, like Jesus, to commit to living a lifestyle of forgiveness by refusing to keep a record of wrongs against anyone, either in your mind or as a written list.

1. Write a few sentences about what it means to you not to keep a record of wrongs. How do you practically do this?

2. If you are sincere about committing to a lifestyle of forgiveness, you may first need to do a little housecleaning! I needed to forgive my father; Shannon, her husband; Claire, an adult child; and Ginger, her mother. Whom do you need to forgive? What hurts remain in your heart because someone has wounded you? Now is the time to let go of your pain. As you do, ponder the truth in this chart:

Forgiveness *Is*	Forgiveness *Is Not*
choosing to keep no record of wrongs	approving of what the person did
refusing to punish the offender	excusing or denying what the person did
giving up your right to talk about the offense in an accusing way	pardoning what the person did
being merciful	reconciling (an exchange between two people)
being gracious	being blind to what happened
the absence of bitterness	forgetting what happened
letting your offender off your hook and releasing them to God's hook	downplaying the hurt of the offense

3. Review what Claire did on page 110. Write all your hurts on a sheet of paper. Ponder it, and surrender it to God. Then rip up the paper and throw it in the trash. Begin your lifestyle of forgiveness today with a clean heart.

4. If God leads, share with your group how you let go of your hurts or any plans you have in the future to keep no record of wrongs. Please remember to respect the privacy of others as you share.

God Forgives Y-O-U

Forgiveness is easier to extend to others when we remember how much God has forgiven us. As Jesus hung on the cross, His last words to His Father included "It is finished." The Greek word used to render this expression is *tetelestai*, which refers to completion or fulfillment. What was finished? The record of your sins was ripped up! You are forgiven!

5. Read Psalm 103:1-14. List at least five gracious, merciful acts of God in these verses. Write a paragraph about how it feels to be clean, to have all your sins wiped away.

6. Read Matthew 18:21-35.

   a. What does Peter ask in Matthew 18:21, and what is Jesus' response? Why do you think Jesus told the parable about the king's wicked servant in response to Peter's question?

   b. What do you observe about the heart of the king in this story?

   c. What is God saying to you through these verses and this parable?

The Hardest Kind of Forgiveness

7. What did you learn from my and Shannon's stories about forgiveness (pages 101–103 and 106–108)? How did forgiving change us?

8. Have you ever had to forgive a parent or an adult child? What was that experience like? If you are comfortable, share how you forgave with the group.

9. What did you feel after reading Ginger's story about forgiving her abusive mother (pages 111–116)?

   a. Do you think Jesus says there's ever a time when someone doesn't deserve forgiveness?

   b. It took years for Ginger to forgive her mom. Why do you think she planned her forgiveness ceremony the way she did?

c. Why do you think it was important for Ginger to have a daily reminder she could see of her decision to forgive?

d. Review the four things Ginger thanked God for on page 116. Which two do you most identify with, and why?

EIGHT-WEEK BIBLE STUDY

Bask in Your Blessings

Congratulations! Did you know that forgiveness comes with a benefits package?

10. Forgiveness can slam the door on Satan! You kick Satan out of your life when you forgive (2 Corinthians 2:10-11). Write thanks to God for this wonderful benefit of forgiving!

11. Forgiveness can bring glory to you! Did you know that forgiving an offense brings you honor (Proverbs 19:11)? Bible scholar Bruce Waltke suggests that the glory a woman receives when she forgives the sin of another is like an "attractive adornment" she wears.[1] How does that make you feel?

12. Spend private and group time in prayer thanking God for what you're learning about forgiveness. Ask Him to continue to speak to you personally about the importance of keeping no record of wrongs.

Forgive Playlist

~ "Forgiveness" by Matthew West
~ "At Your Feet" by Casting Crowns

WEEK 7

Encourage

Heart Skill
A HIDING PLACE

David's hiding place was first a spiritual destination, a safe refuge where his mind, heart, and spirit went to be alone with God. Second, it was a physical location, his granite fortress or other places that David went to be alone with God to commune with Him on a heart level. Write a paragraph, a psalm, or a poem (or make a collage or an acrostic) that describes your hiding place in God.

Your Personal Hiding Place

A Spiritual Destination

Psalm 46:10 says, "Be still, and know that I am God." Spend between fifteen minutes to an hour with the Father, who longs to speak to you. To open your time, listen to "Quiet Places" by Shannon Adducci (see the QR code at the end of this section). Ask God to talk to you about how you can hide yourself under the shadow of His wing and in His holy presence.

1. Record any thoughts, ideas, phrases, or pictures that the Lord showed you as you were quiet before Him. If you feel comfortable, share with your group.

A Physical Location

A hiding place is also a physical location. Here are some of the hideaways different women have told me they have found:

- ~ "I turned a little closet into my hideout, and it has become my all-time favorite place with God."
- ~ "I take a daily walk that leads to a hiding place in the woods where I can kneel alone, away from everyone and everything."
- ~ "My hiding place is nothing special to look at—it's my favorite chair in my bedroom. But, oh, I've had some really holy moments in that chair."
- ~ "I place lots of big pillows on the far side of our bed on the floor and nestle down in them where no one can find me, and I'm alone with my God."

2. Share with your group about where you go to meet with God. If you don't have a hiding place yet, which place out of the four mentioned above most appeals to you, and why?

Encouragement on the Spot

3. None of us like discouragement! Describe a time the devil tried to use his tool of discouragement on you and how you responded.

4. Read 1 Samuel 30:1-18. Focus on verse 6. Have you experienced encouraging yourself in the Lord? What did this look like for you? Share with your group.

As we look at Psalm 19, we see four major ways David encouraged himself in the Lord:

~ creation
~ Scripture
~ worship
~ a hiding place

Creation

5. Read Psalm 19:1-6. Think about David with the sheep on the hillside. Walk outside at night and look at the starry sky with new eyes. Write a paragraph praising God for His heavens.

Scripture

6. Read Psalm 19:7-14 and discover all that the Word of God can be to you! Pray the prayer at the end of Psalm 19, and ask God to search your heart. List some of the ways God's Word instructs you.

Worship

Read Psalm 63. As you read, remember that David wrote this as he was fleeing from his son Absalom, who wanted to kill him.

7. List at least three ways worship deepens your intimacy with the Lord.

A Hiding Place

Psalm 63 can be divided like this:

- ~ Psalm 63:1-4 describes God as the desire of my being.
- ~ Psalm 63:5-8 describes God as the delight of my soul.
- ~ Psalm 63:9-11 describes God as the defense of my life.

8. How do you think it would help you make God your hiding place if you knew that He were all these things?

Encouragement in the Long Struggle

9. It's hard to imagine what we would do if our lives began to *CRACK!* like Crystal and Doug's. What did you learn from their story?

10. What was the main truth about making God your hiding place and refuge that you learned from Crystal and Doug?

11. Read John 7:37-38. How has the Living Water of the Holy Spirit poured through Crystal and Doug? How have you seen this Living Water pour through you?

Encouragement Flows Forward

12. Read 2 Corinthians 1:3-4. How have you seen God bring comfort and encouragement to you and then let it flow out to others?

13. Whom is God asking you to encourage?

Encourage Playlist

~ "Quiet Places" by Shannon Adducci
~ "Creator" by Phil Wickham
~ "Word of God Speak" by MercyMe
~ "You Are My Hiding Place" by Selah

EIGHT-WEEK BIBLE STUDY

WEEK 8
Praise

Heart Skill
A PRACTICE

Begin your own holy habit of praising God daily. Spend at least thirty minutes alone with God, and ask Him what names of His have been important to you over the years. Look at Valerie's list (page 153). Then select seven to ten different names of God and praise Him with these names out loud every day.

1. After prayerfully choosing your list of names, write them in the space below. Share the names with your group and why you chose them.

2. Consider how you can incorporate teaching the ABCs of God's names to your children or grandchildren or with a friend. Write here how you might do this.

Valerie's Praise Practice

3. Valerie declared God's names to Him twice and sometimes three times a day. She said that doing this refreshed her soul and enabled her to feel God's power at work in her life. Did you feel any different this week after speaking God's names out loud to Him? If so, what did you notice?

4. Valerie said that praise and pain can coexist. Have you found this true in your own life? If so, how?

5. Valerie's praise practice inspired a woman named Darlene to sit by a lake for three hours declaring the names of God. These holy names evoked excitement, joy, delight, and peace in her soul. Here are a few names that emerged from her meditations:

My Abba Father
My Beloved
My Counselor
The Deliverer
Emmanuel
My Best Friend
The Gentle Healer
The I Am That I Am
The Just One
Living Water

God may want to surprise you with some of His names when you are alone with Him as well!

Daniel's Praise Practice

6. Daniel's practice of bowing before God seemed to be at specific times of the day. Are there certain activities or breaks that you have every day that would create space for you to praise God?

7. Read Daniel 2:19-23. What do you learn about Daniel from this prayer? What do you learn about God?

Your Praise Practice

Your personal practice of praise can look different depending on your season of life and unique personality. As you develop your praise practice, reflect on what each of these women have discovered. We can learn from one another!

8. When Lorraine drove her kids to school, they had to wait five minutes each day for the train to cross the tracks. The train stop was a signal for Lorraine and her daughters, who knew this was their "thank-you time to God." What stops are a part of your life that you can use to praise God?

9. Music is Alia's praise outlet. She runs for thirty minutes three times a week and uses this time to sing and worship God. What praise outlet fills your heart, and how can you incorporate it into your daily or weekly rhythms?

10. Mae loves to write. Every Monday she looks back over the past week and makes a long praise list in her journal. What would you put in a praise list for this week?

11. I love nature. When I walk my dog for thirty minutes each day, I breathe in the fresh air and praise God for His beautiful creation as I look at the Colorado mountains. When it rains and turns the high desert green, I thank Him for much-needed moisture. What elements of nature cause you to praise God?

12. No one led a busier life than Jesus. He was a man who never stopped doing whatever the Father had for Him to do, yet He still felt the need to spend time alone . . . much time alone with His Abba. Read the following verses and note the ways and times He spent time with His Father: Mark 1:35; Luke 5:16; and John 12:27-30.

Your Eight Heart Skills

13. At the beginning of this study, we talked about *hokmah*, the Hebrew word for "wisdom" that's often understood as "skill." This wisdom is not based on human reasoning but on the supernatural wisdom that the Holy Spirit weaves into your life. How have you seen your wisdom grow as you've read this book and prayerfully sought God's presence in this season of your life?

14. Think back on each of the Heart Skills you've sought to incorporate into your life. Of all these Heart Skills, which have impacted you the most, and why?

Chapter	Heart Skill	Method
Hope	a declaration	a statement/symbol/decree that expresses your hope in God
Love	a plan	a spiritual workout plan designed to deepen your intimacy with God
Loss	a journal	writing daily in a Thankful Journal to help maintain perspective about your loss
Lament	a lament	a written prayer that expresses your sorrow to God
Trust	a verse (or verses)	a life verse or passage that expresses your trust in God
Forgive	a lifestyle	a choice not to keep a record of wrongs
Encourage	a hiding place	finding your spiritual and physical hiding place in God
Praise	a practice	a daily praise practice of declaring the names of God

Praise Playlist

- "The Hallelujah Chorus" from George Frideric Handel's *Messiah*
- "Raise a Hallelujah" by Jonathan and Melissa Helser (Bethel Music)
- "A Thousand Hallelujahs" by Brooke Ligertwood

ACKNOWLEDGMENTS

I began writing when I was thirty-four, and I am now eighty-two. Writing this book is the most difficult thing I have ever tried to do. Why? Because it is so personal and tells of my pain and shattered dreams. Many people have encouraged me along the way, and I want to thank them for lifting me up.

To Nancy Petak, the giving leader of the twelve women from The Ascent Church in Monument, Colorado, and Mindy King, the amazing Zoom leader of the Abide Sisters from four US time zones and Canada. I shout "Hurrah!" for your extremely helpful input. Because of your suggestions, one chapter was rewritten, one Heart Skill changed, and many Bible-study questions redone. Your help was invaluable. THANK YOU!

To Ginger, Crystal, Shannon, Valerie, and the many others who graciously shared your stories, poems, and laments to bring hope to hurting hearts. Bless you, my sisters.

Special thanks to the amazing team at NavPress! It is such a privilege to work with you! Thank you, David, for your leadership, and Caitlyn, for not only being an excellent editor but also for listening, caring, and making time. Elizabeth, your expertise is appreciated, and yours, too, Danielle! And Julie, amazing cover designer who seeks God for the design. Thank you!

To Terry Behimer, the special friend who said, "I'll be your agent because you need one." What a friend you are! Your input is all over this book. Thank you!

To my two special daughters: Joy Michelle DuPuis and Robin Grace Happonen, sisters and best friends. I thank God for the privilege of being your mother, mommy, mom, and mutti—and watching you both be such amazing mothers to your own daughters.

NOTES

DOES YOUR LIFE HURT?
1. Walter Bauer and William F. Arndt, *A Greek-English Lexicon of the New Testament and Other Early Christian Literature*, 3rd ed., ed. Frederick W. Danker (Chicago: University of Chicago Press, 2000), 219.
2. R. Laird Harris, Gleason L. Archer Jr., and Bruce K. Waltke, eds., *Theological Wordbook of the Old Testament* (Chicago: Northfield Publishing, 1999), 283. *Hokmah* ("wisdom") refers to godly cleverness and skill that results in practical action. The one who hears (Proverbs 8:33; 23:19; 27:11) will be industrious and will know how to talk, and his will will be in captivity to God's.

CHAPTER 1 | HOPE
1. Lawrence O. Richards, *Expository Dictionary of Bible Words* (Grand Rapids: Zondervan, 1985, 1991), 344.
2. Timothy Keller, *Walking with God through Pain and Suffering* (New York: Riverhead, 2015), 289.
3. See, for example, Tammy Kennington, "How to Discover Hope When Seeds of Promises Are Unfulfilled," *Hope Restored* (blog), August 5, 2022, https://tammykennington.com/how-to-discover-hope-when-seeds-of-promises-are-unfulfilled.
4. Mark Vroegop, *Dark Clouds, Deep Mercy: Discovering the Grace of Lament* (Wheaton, IL: Crossway, 2019), 111.
5. Richards, *Expository Dictionary of Bible Words*, 576.

6. Terry Wardle, *Draw Close to the Fire: Finding God in the Darkness* (Abilene, TX: Leafwood Publishers, 2004), 62.

CHAPTER 2 | LOVE
1. Leon Morris, *The First Epistle of Paul to the Corinthians: An Introduction and Commentary* (London: InterVarsity Press, 1985), 177.
2. H. A. Ironside, *Addresses on the First Epistle to the Corinthians* (Neptune, NJ: Loizeaux Brothers, 1938), 424.
3. C. S. Lewis, *The Problem of Pain* (New York: Collier Books, 1962), 93.
4. A. W. Tozer, *The Divine Conquest* (Old Tappan, NJ: Revell, 1950), 26.
5. Charles Haddon Spurgeon, *The Treasury of David: Spurgeon's Great Commentary on the Book of Psalms* (Nashville: Thomas Nelson, 1998), 1420, https://www.blueletterbible.org/Comm/spurgeon_charles/tod/ps139.cfm.
6. Vanessa Calys-Tagoe, "Jacqueline Kiplimo, The Kenyan Athlete Who Gave up First Place to Help an Armless Chinese," *Face2Face Africa*, September 6, 2022, https://face2faceafrica.com/article/acqueline-kiplimo-the-kenyan-athlete-who-gave-up-first-place-to-help-an-armless-chinese.

CHAPTER 3 | LOSS
1. Conferences based on the book *Intimate Issues: 21 Questions Christian Women Ask about Sex* (Colorado Springs: WaterBrook Press, 1999) by Linda Dillow and Lorraine Pintus.
2. Thank you to Bob Sorge for writing about the "toughest verse in the Bible" and the "fattest promise" in the Bible in his excellent book *Between the Lines: God Is Writing Your Story* (Kansas City, MO: Oasis House, 2012).
3. Sorge, *Between the Lines*, 63.
4. Sorge, *Between the Lines*, 64.
5. Zane Hodges, *The Epistle of James: Proven Character through Testing: A Verse by Verse Commentary* (Irving, TX: Grace Evangelical Society, 1994), 26.
6. See, for example, J. Sidlow Baxter, *Explore the Book: A Survey and Study of Each Book from Genesis to Revelation* (Grand Rapids: Zondervan, 1966), 285.
7. Neil R. Coulter, "Dr. Daniel Wallace: The Worshipful Call to Learning, Teaching, and Learning Again," *Voice: Dallas Theological Seminary Magazine* (Fall 2022), https://voice.dts.edu/article/daniel-wallace-the-worshipful-call.
8. Coulter, "Dr. Daniel Wallace."
9. Joni Eareckson Tada, *Infinite Hope in the Midst of Struggles* (Carol Stream, IL: Tyndale House Publishers, 2018), 116.
10. Jerry Sittser, *A Grace Disguised: How the Soul Grows through Loss* (Grand Rapids: Zondervan, 2004), 17.

NOTES

CHAPTER 4 | LAMENT

1. Anni, "Annika's Lament," in *Remedies* (Thousand Oaks, CA: Aslon Press, 2024), 72. Annika's nickname is Anni.
2. Donna Fagerstrom, *Every Mourning* (Plano, TX: MPACT Communications, 2017), 15.
3. Mark Vroegop, *Dark Clouds, Deep Mercy: Discovering the Grace of Lament* (Wheaton, IL: Crossway, 2019), 28.
4. Mark Vroegop, "6 Reasons Christians Need to Learn to Lament," Crossway, April 7, 2019, https://www.crossway.org/articles/6-reasons-christians-need-to-learn-to-lament.
5. Timothy Keller, *Walking with God through Pain and Suffering* (New York: Riverhead, 2015), 241.
6. Michael Card, *A Sacred Sorrow: Reaching Out to God in the Lost Language of Lament* (Colorado Springs: NavPress, 2005), 7.
7. Matt Redman, "Matt Redman - Son of Suffering (Lyric Video)," *Homecoming*, Integrity Music, 2021. Premiered Live October 7, 2022, from Mission San Juan Capistrano. YouTube video, 7:34, https://www.youtube.com/watch?v=Uf3xjglSKQc.
8. Other translations handle the ambiguous original language in Psalm 77:10 differently than the NASB. In his excellent commentary, James Montgomery Boice offers four possibilities for translation: "This is my appeal: the years of the right hand of the Most High"; "This is my grief: the years of the right hand of the Most High"; "This is my grief: the right hand of the Most High has changed"; and "This is my appeal: the right hand of the Most High has changed." James Montgomery Boice, *Psalms Volume 2: Psalms 42–106*, An Expositional Commentary (Ada, MI: Baker Books, 1996), 641.
9. Vroegop, *Dark Clouds*, 112.
10. Listen to this beautiful worship song by Shannon Adducci that is also a mom's lament: "He Loves You More," *Loved*, Shanny Banny Music, 2023, YouTube video, 4:27, https://youtu.be/mabI-UJItFs.
11. Edited from an excerpt by Michael Card, *A Sacred Sorrow*, 114–15.
12. Anni, "I'm Getting to Know You," *Remedies*, 92.

CHAPTER 5 | TRUST

1. See, for example, Walter Bauer and William F. Arndt, *A Greek-English Lexicon of the New Testament and Other Early Christian Literature*, 3rd ed., ed. Frederick W. Danker (Chicago: University of Chicago Press, 2000), 819.
2. Jerry Bridges, *Trusting God: Even When Life Hurts* (Colorado Springs: NavPress, 2008), 18.

3. F. B. Meyer, as quoted in Mrs. Charles E. Cowman, *Streams in the Desert* (Grand Rapids: Zondervan, 1925), 23.
4. David Guzik, *Enduring Word Bible Commentary*, "Habakkuk 1," https://enduringword.com/bible-commentary/habakkuk-1.
5. In the years since writing "Blessings," God has blessed Laura and Martin Story with four beautiful children.
6. Laura Story, "Blessings," *Blessings*, INO Records, 2011, YouTube video, 4:59, https://www.youtube.com/watch?v=JKPeoPiK9XE.
7. Laura Story, *When God Doesn't Fix It: Lessons You Never Wanted to Learn, Truths You Can't Live Without* (Nashville: W Publishing Group, 2015), 133.
8. Story, *When God Doesn't Fix It*, 143.
9. For more on Alaine's story, see Alaine Pakkala, *Taking Every Thought Captive: Spiritual Workouts to Help Renew Your Mind in God's Truth* (Colorado Springs: Lydia Press, 1995).
10. Linda Dillow and Dr. Juli Slattery, *Surprised by the Healer: Embracing Hope for Your Broken Story* (Chicago: Moody, 2016), 163–64.
11. Christina Rossetti, "A Christmas Carol," *The Century Illustrated Monthly Magazine*, vol. 3 (1871–1872, Nov.–Apr.), ed. J. G. Holland (New York: Scribner, 1872). Public domain.

CHAPTER 6 | FORGIVENESS
1. I know this is a difficult word, but I fought to include it because the shock and brutality of it has echoed throughout my life, and I know some of you have felt the same way. I apologize if it's offensive and hurtful to you, but please know it was, and is, to me also.
2. "What Is Forgiveness?" *Greater Good Magazine*, Greater Good Science Center, University of California, Berkeley, https://greatergood.berkeley.edu/topic/forgiveness/definition.
3. Charles R. Swindoll, *Growing Strong in the Seasons of Life* (Grand Rapids: Zondervan, 1994), 193.
4. The names in this story have been changed, but the story is true. Good news! Four years after Claire shared this, she said, "Nathan is out of prison. He has turned his life over to Jesus. While he still deals with mental-health issues from the years of drug abuse, we do a Bible study together every Saturday morning."

CHAPTER 7 | ENCOURAGEMENT
1. Various versions of this story can be found online. Author unknown.
2. *Dis-* (Latin), meaning "away." Dictionary.com, s.v. "dis-," accessed July 31, 2024, https://www.dictionary.com/browse/dis.
3. *Collins Dictionary*, s.v. "en-," accessed July 31, 2024, https://www.collinsdictionary.com/dictionary/english/en. "*En-* is added to words to

NOTES

form verbs that describe the process of putting someone into a particular state, condition, or place."
4. Lawrence O. Richards, *Expository Dictionary of Bible Words* (Grand Rapids: Zondervan, 1985, 1991), 247.
5. Other resources indicate that David may also have had the books of Joshua and Judges.
6. Since Doug can't speak, I emailed this question to Crystal and Doug, and they replied.
7. Max Lucado, *It's Not about Me: Rescue from the Life We Thought Would Make Us Happy* (Nashville: Thomas Nelson, 2004), 125.
8. Lucado, *It's Not about Me*, 127.
9. See, for example, Steven Lawson, "Luther and the Psalms: His Solace and Strength" (October 15, 2012), https://www.ligonier.org/learn/articles/luther-and-psalms-his-solace-and-strength.
10. Lawrence J. Crabb Jr. and Dan B. Allender, *Encouragement: The Key to Caring* (Grand Rapids, Zondervan, 1984), 20.

CHAPTER 8 | PRAISE
1. Some of the factual information in this section is adapted from Jack R. Taylor, *The Hallelujah Factor* (Nashville: Broadman Press, 1983), 80.
2. Taylor Haney, Reena Advani, and Leila Fadel, National Public Radio (NPR) (KRCC), "Taken by Russia, then Rescued, Young Ukrainians Speak Out" (February 8, 2024), https://www.npr.org/202402/08/1228453066/taken-by-russia-then-rescued-young-ukrainians-speak-out.
3. Charles C. Ryrie, *The Ryrie Study Bible*, New American Standard Bible (Chicago: Moody, 1978), 1307 (footnote commentary on Daniel 1:7).

EIGHT-WEEK BIBLE STUDY
1. Bruce K. Waltke, *The Book of Proverbs, Chapters 15–31*, New International Commentary on the Old Testament (Grand Rapids: Eerdmans, 2005), 105.

MORE FROM LINDA DILLOW

GREAT FOR GROUP READS—EACH BOOK INCLUDES A PLAN SO IT CAN BE USED FOR GROUP STUDY

CALM my ANXIOUS HEART
LINDA DILLOW

SATISFY my THIRSTY SOUL
LINDA DILLOW

a DEEPER KIND OF CALM
LINDA DILLOW

NavPress
Bold. Loving. Sensible.™

Available at NavPress.com and wherever books are sold.

NavPress
Bold. Loving. Sensible.™

Since 1975, NavPress, a business ministry of The Navigators, has been producing books, ministry resources, and *The Message* Bible to help people to know Christ, make Him known, and help others do the same.®

> "God doesn't want us to be shy with his gifts, but bold and loving and sensible."
> 2 Timothy 1:7, *The Message*

Learn more about NavPress:

Learn more about The Navigators:

Find NavPress on social media: